笑酒

izakaya

シンスケ 山利喜 尋

buchi

i z a k a y a

THE JAPANESE PUB COOKBOOK

MARK ROBINSON

PHOTOGRAPHS BY Masashi Kuma

KODANSHA INTERNATIONAL
Tokyo • New York • London

Distributed in the United States by Kodansha America LLC, and in the United
Kingdom and continental Europe by Kodansha Europe Ltd.

Published by Kodansha International Ltd., 17-14 Otowa 1-chome, Bunkyo-ku,
Tokyo 112-8652.

ISBN 978-4-7700-3065-8

First edition, 2008
18 17 16 15 14 13 12 11 10 09   15 14 13 12 11 10 9 8 7 6 5

        Library of Congress Cataloging-in-Publication Data

Robinson, Mark.
 Izakaya : the Japanese pub cookbook / by Mark Robinson ; photographs by
Masashi Kuma.
    p. cm.
 Includes index.
 ISBN 978-4-7700-3065-8
 1. Cookery, Japanese. I. Title.
 TX724.5.J3R63 2008
 641.5952--dc22
                        2007045650

www.kodansha-intl.com

Contents

INTRODUCTION 6

Horoyoi ∎ LAUGHING DRUNK ——————————— 10

Maru ∎ MASTER CLASS ——————————— 30

IZAKAYA HISTORY ——————————— 48

Saiki ∎ DREAM ON ——————————— 50

JAPANESE AROMATICS ——————————— 66

Shinsuke ∎ TIME AND AGAIN ——————————— 70

Yamariki ∎ GUTS ——————————— 86

IZAKAYA DRINKING ——————————— 102

Hiro ∎ TRADITIONAL RADICAL ——————————— 106

Morimoto ∎ LOVE OF THE GAME ——————————— 122

Buchi ∎ FUTURE PERFECT ——————————— 134

TALKING IZAKAYA 152
GLOSSARY 153
INDEX 156
MAPS 159
ACKNOWLEDGMENTS and SOURCES 160

Once in a Lifetime

During my research for this book, I took two friends to one of my favorite pubs on the outskirts of Tokyo, a boisterous, working-class establishment run by a jolly staff of mature women. We sat at a large table beside a tired-looking, elderly businessman who was reading a book over his beer, and ordered, among other dishes, breaded pork and onion skewers, horse mackerel *sashimi*, grated *daikon* radish with baby sardines, and a potato salad. After an hour or so, the businessman said hello, and we asked him what he was reading. He raised his book to show us. It was *Henry V*, in Japanese. I noticed that he had taken a fluorescent highlighter pen to many passages. He beamed and said, "But who I really like is Falstaff!" referring to the gluttonous, comic drunk of *Henry IV*. Then he raised his hand in a drinking gesture and said, "Glug, glug, glug."

On the face of it, it was an unremarkable incident, but it has stayed with me. Somehow, this weary corporate employee with his enthusiasm for Shakespeare and the drive to enjoy it in a noisy neighborhood pub changed the complexion of the room. It was a fleeting point of deep contact, and it made our evening. It was the sort of thing that often happens at the Japanese pub, a case of what is known as *ichigo ichie*—or "once in a lifetime," and it reminded me again of why I wanted to write this book.

Since I moved to Tokyo in the late 1980s, the *izakaya* (pronounced roughly ee-ZAH-ka-ya), has provided me with a consistently comforting, authentic, and thrilling-to-my-Western-visitors food experience. I believe that the izakaya is overdue to become one of the biggest Japanese cuisine trends abroad since the sushi bar.

For too long there has been a misperception about Japanese food: that it is uniformly finicky, requires years of training to produce, is steeped in rules and ritual, and hence has to be expensive—and not especially fun. Nothing could be further from the truth. I know dozens of Japanese who have never set foot in a *kaiseki* haute cuisine restaurant, and many who have never eaten top-grade sushi. But I know no Japanese of drinking age

The *noren* curtain at the entrance of Maru.

who has not enjoyed an izakaya. And—in most cases—at prices surprisingly below the Western restaurant equivalent.

Neither restaurant nor bar, the izakaya is more than a place where you can share delicious food and relaxing drink—though it is certainly that. In many neighborhoods, it is a community hub with a cast of characters and ongoing narratives. The customers will range from locals and regulars to office workers, academics or day-laborers. They will order small-dish delicacies throughout the evening, perhaps in the beginning sharing just a couple of items. The menu is like a road map and the diners are at the wheel, calling out orders as the mood takes them. All dishes are inexpensive, and as the "scenery" and conversation changes, items that initially escaped notice acquire new appeal. No inquisitive diner can fail to broaden his or her horizons, wandering side routes into exciting new food avenues. And as the evening progresses and energy levels rise, you will hear straight talk and the uttering of hard truths that won't ordinarily be spoken. In short, at the izakaya, people are more themselves.

MY INTENTION in writing this book is twofold: one, to describe and evoke as best I can the izakaya food culture, and secondly, to pass on some recipes that I find delicious and reassuring: recipes that don't appear elsewhere, and allow you to recreate a Japanese pub meal at home, whether for a party or a simple dinner.

Izakaya come in countless forms to suit all tastes, from the down-home working-class pub to the chic designer establishment, and I have tried to cover the entire experience. The establishments I have included represent a cross-section of what to me are some of Tokyo's best establishments, and I have taken "izakaya" as an umbrella term that includes a *yakitori* barbecue chicken pub which, strictly speaking, is a separate sort of specialty store, although the eating style is the same, and certainly just as enjoyable.

Deferring to the ubiquity of its usage, I have also adopted the most common English translation of izakaya—"pub"—while recognizing its sheer inadequacy to describe the experience.

Regarding the recipes: the izakaya masters who so generously shared them with me were sometimes perplexed when asked to write them down, or describe them in terms of specific quantities of ingredients and seasonings. It is hardly surprising that for chefs who know their craft backward and forward, cooking via measurements such as half cups and teaspoons is an alien concept. I have tried to recreate these dishes as closely as possible, but stress that the most important aspect of cooking with delicate *dashi* stocks and simple ingredients is to taste as you go. One should adjust cooking times to allow for the many variations in fattiness, toughness or water content of the meat, fish or vegetables you are using. But it all comes down to this: the overriding rule of Japanese cuisine is that the produce you use must be as fresh as you can find, and the simpler the recipe, the better it must be. (Recipe measurements are U.S.)

On serving sizes, it is impossible to say exactly how many portions most of these recipes yield. (This is also the beauty of izakaya eating, as diners may enjoy as much or as little as they like.) But to give a rough guide, in most cases I have estimated each recipe to be one of a selection of four to six dishes to be shared among a small group.

AN UNFAMILIAR izakaya can be daunting to enter, and this goes as much for the Japanese as anyone. Unlike your average restaurant, with its tables in the window to attract passing trade, the izakaya, with its frosted glass door obscuring the action, and mysterious, hanging *noren* curtain outside, is almost the reverse. But you have nothing to lose if, when passing such an establishment, upon noticing the hanging lantern and the drifting chatter and aromas, you gently stick your head inside, hold up a few fingers to indicate the number in your group and step into a new adventure.

If you have little Japanese language, order by gesturing to what other patrons are enjoying, or ask for some of the dishes in this book. In the relaxed atmosphere of the quality izakaya you will easily make friends, and come away inspired by a night that will never be repeated.

LAUGHING
DRUNK

酒笑 Horoyoi

Every neighborhood deserves a Horoyoi. Amid the babble of nighttime Ebisu, southwestern Tokyo, among the mind-numbing array of flashy restaurants dueling for customers, their touts plying the streets, this diminutive semi-basement izakaya has been a fixture in my life since the early 1990s.

I never consciously made it so. Indeed, it was some years before I realized that Horoyoi had grown on me—or I had grown into it—to the extent that I relied on it as much as the average Japanese might his or her own "local": as a modest, welcoming place that came instantly to mind when arranging to eat and drink with friends and colleagues; to casually celebrate birthdays and New Year's; to entertain relatives; or to introduce newcomers to izakaya. Over time, I found that it had transcended its status as an occasional destination to become a regular venue for marking some of my life's milestones: a personal repository of good memories. With its minimal décor, reliable, simply seasoned food and cool-headed service, it was a place where I felt at the same time comfortably well known and sufficiently anonymous to be completely myself. I could bring whomever I pleased, stay as long or short as I wanted, ask questions about the menu, be gregarious, or simply sit and observe. And that's what the best neighborhood izakaya should be.

Go down the few stairs from the street into the narrow L-shaped room, squeezing past the cash register, *sake* fridge and beer kegs, turning sideways to negotiate the jutting limbs of patrons seated along the timber-paneled wall, and take a ringside stool at the counter, among the piles of liquor bottles and crockery. Nod good evening to lanky chef Nobuhiro Ando and his stocky deputy, Yuko Kawamura, who will likely return to you the same deadpan shrug with which they have greeted me for years. Peer over the refrigerated *sashimi* cabinet and observe how in an open kitchen barely large enough to turn around in, they juggle the rapid construction of an extensive menu of small-plate dishes: cutting, braising, broiling or peeling; deep frying savory stuffed peppers or tofu; whipping together seaweed salads; or performing surgical procedures on fish. The action is soothing to watch, and if Ando and Kawamura are men of few words (though they will gladly chat about their food as they work) their silence is one of confidence, for they barely need to speak.

The routine at Horoyoi is innovative: each of the men spends two weeks as chef, then two weeks working the floor with the waitress, leaping into the kitchen at peak times to assist. Orders shouted by diners are met with an abrupt "*Hai*" of affirmation as either Ando or Kawamura starts prepping, while the other digs out ingredients. "We make a good team," Ando tells me. He has worked here since 1989, and Kawamura joined about eight years later. "Kawamura can cook almost anything, so we take turns. If you don't make the food yourself you don't know what's needed from the fridge without being told—that's the good thing about swapping roles."

So . . . what to order? The basic menu com-prises almost one hundred items over ten categories, and includes Small Dishes, Salads, Fried Foods, Hotpots, Grilled Dishes, Tempura, Rice Dishes, and others. On top of these are twenty or so daily specials of sashimi, shellfish, and other seasonal items on a separate menu printed out every evening from the pub's laptop computer. Little circles made in red felt-tip pen mark the recommendations—starting from the top right-hand corner with sashimi (with which most patrons begin)—and a small blackboard menu lists the picks of these.

On a typical night in early spring, it includes simmered bamboo shoots, salt-grilled *ayu* sweetfish, yellowtail sashimi, and raw *hotaru ika* firefly squid, with a sweet white miso dressing. The ingredients are provided daily by Horoyoi's owner whose main business is wholesaling produce. You might run into him should you arrive very early—and mistake him for the delivery man—an elderly gentleman dressed in parka and auction bidder's cap, arms laden with vegetables and fish. As far as Horoyoi is concerned, he leaves almost all decisions to Ando, and for a long time I never knew of his existence.

VISITING IZAKAYA alone has its specific charms, but the obvious advantage of attending a place like this with friends is that you can sample a much broader range of delicious food, and given Horoyoi's sprawling selection, that's what I recommend here. If there are too many of you to chat comfortably at the counter, the *zashiki* floor-seating area at the back of the room is where you should head (provided your knees can take it), to sit on thin cushions around the low tables. You should, of course, remove your shoes before stepping up (note the provision of vinyl slippers, to wear to the bathroom). One of the staff will immediately be with you, proffering a hot handtowel and asking for your drink order.

What might be seen by the leisurely Western diner as pushy behavior—asking your order when you are barely seated—is a custom which stems from the fact that most izakaya patrons know what they want to drink—and they want it straight away. If you wish to ponder the extensive list of sake and *shochu* distilled spirits, you will probably ask for a *toriaezu biiru* ("for-the-time-being beer"), so that everyone in the group can kick off the evening promptly.

The characters chosen to write Horoyoi translate as "laughingly drunk," and it's an appropriate name since the izakaya opened in 1984, when Japan was emerging from the *jizake* boom, a huge spike in popularity of regional, minor sake brewers. Horoyoi's boast was its exceptional range of such drink, and still today the centerpiece of the pub is the huge, green, backlit screen, showing a map of Japan dotted with sake bottles at their geographical origins. The shelves above the zashiki area struggle to support scores of giant brown, 1.8 liter (half-gallon) bottles, but in a sign of changing times, the majority of them contain not sake but shochu. "In the old days our drink sales were pretty much all sake, and only a fifth shochu," Ando tells me. "No one drank *imo* [sweet potato] shochu, it had a cheap image and was a bit of a joke. But now it makes up about half our sales. People think it's good for you. Especially women."

Women are driving other changes: they are turning up in increasing numbers—and without men. Ando is somewhat incredulous. "This is a typical izakaya, the sort of place you associate only with older men," he says.

"It's nothing fancy, you might almost say it's unwelcoming for women. But we often have young women coming in or making phone reservations." He laughs. "They research on the Internet; someone has a good impression, and blogs about us."

ON THIS NIGHT, much like many others, I take a seat at the end of the counter, ask for a draft beer and examine the fresh fish in the low refrigerated glass cabinet. I order a grilled surf clam and some *katsuo* bonito sashimi. The pub is almost full, and the noise level is at a relaxed din. The customers range from their twenties to sixties, and the steady buzz of conversation is impassioned and cheerful, while the occasional emphatic remark meets an outburst of laughter. At one table against the far wall, two white-shirted young businessmen are locked in earnest conversation, allowing each other time to speak before responding after a thoughtful period. Between them are the remains of a whole grilled squid sprinkled with finely chopped *aonegi* green onions, a plate of homemade potato chips, another fried dish, and the leftovers of something raw. On the wall above them, stretching to the front door, is a row of sake brands hand painted on thin strips of cedar. Directly behind me is the zashiki area, as wide as the store—about sixteen feet—and raised about one foot. It is populated by chatty men and women, half of whom seem to belong to the same corporation.

In front of me, Ando works methodically as the requests flow in, while Kawamura crisscrosses the floor, serving and taking orders. When a middle-aged businessman and his female companion occupy the seats beside me and order horse mackerel sashimi, Ando takes a small fishing net such as those used for tropical aquariums and scoops a feisty six-inch fish out of the glass tank at the opposite end of the counter. Before the fish knows what is happening, Ando has clean-filleted one side and flipped it over, still flapping, to repeat the action. He puts it aside and skins and bones the fillets, slices them delicately, then picks up the fish—now just a head, tail, and skein of flesh on a cartoon-like skeleton—and impales it in an "S" shape on a thin wooden skewer, before laying it onto a diamond-shaped plate and arranging the sashimi pieces on top.

He garnishes it with white shredded *daikon* radish, a green *shiso* leaf and yellow grated ginger, sprinkles it with *aonegi* green onions and places it on the counter for the waitress to serve. The fish twitches electrically beside me as my neighbors mix their ginger into soy sauce before dipping the pieces and eating. The quivering carcass attracts the attention of the two young women on the couple's far side, who stare at it briefly with dazed fascination, then return to their conversation, food, drinks, and cigarettes. It is an explicit display of life and death in the food chain, and a dish no one who prefers to remain removed from it should order.

But always, at Horoyoi, there are myriad delicious alternatives. The hit dish as I write is *atsu-atsu poteeto chippu*, or hot potato chips. It is thin-sliced potatoes, deep-fried and sprinkled with salt. Ando says many diners order two servings. It seems to be a money-maker, so I suggest he raise the price from its cheap ¥400. "How can I?" he splutters. "It's just a potato, sliced and fried!" I know many establishments that would happily charge more for less, but Ando's blunt honesty is surely one factor in this pub's unpretentious appeal.

Chilled Tofu

High in protein and cooling to eat, this simple izakaya classic gets a peppery zing from grated ginger and *daikon* radish sprouts. Give it the slightest splash of soy sauce when serving. *Recipe p. 16*

Vinegared *Wakame* Salad

A mineral-rich salad that is mildly sweet, sour, and redolent of the ocean. The point of the *jabara* "accordion-cut" cucumber is that it holds the delicious vinegar dressing within its pleats. *Recipe p. 16*

Chilled Tofu

冷や奴
Hiyayakko

SERVES 4   P. 14

1 block well chilled silken soft tofu, about 12½ oz. (350g)
¼ cup thinly sliced scallions
A large handful bonito flakes (*katsuo kezuri-bushi*)
2 tsp. grated fresh ginger
Daikon radish sprouts (*kaiware*), optional
Soy sauce

Taking care not to break it, remove the tofu from its container and lay on a paper-lined cutting board. Cut into 12 pieces and arrange in a serving bowl. Arrange daikon sprouts on top of the tofu, sprinkle with the scallions and bonito flakes, and top with grated ginger. Drizzle with soy sauce immediately before eating.

Vinegared *Wakame* Salad

わかめ酢
Wakame-su

SERVES 4   P. 14

1¾ oz. (50g) salted wakame or about ½ oz. (15g) dried wakame
½ Japanese cucumber, accordion-cut (*jabara*) *see Step 3

Sanbaizu Dressing
⌈ 4 tbsp. rice vinegar
  4 tbsp. *dashi* stock *recipe p. 101
  2 tbsp. soy sauce
⌊ 1 tbsp. *mirin*

4 lemon wedges
Daikon radish sprouts (*kaiware*), optional

1. If using salted wakame, remove excess salt by soaking in cold water for 3–5 minutes. For dried wakame, rehydrate following the instructions on the package. Some cooks like to blanch wakame after soaking, for a greener color. Do not soak or blanch for too long, as the wakame will become jelly-like. Lightly squeeze excess water from the wakame, neatly fold and cut into bite-size pieces. Trim away any tough parts.
2. For the sanbaizu dressing: mix all ingredients and bring to a simmer to evaporate the alcohol and sharpness of the vinegar. Immediately remove from heat and let cool to room temperature.
3. For the jabara-cut cucumber: Lay the cucumber on a cutting board and make paper-thin cuts at a 20-degree angle, as if julienning, but to no deeper than the center of the cucumber. Turn over and repeat (these cuts will now run in the opposite direction). Lightly sprinkle with salt and leave until softened (about 20 minutes.) Cut the cucumber into 1½ in. (3.75cm) lengths and twist gently by hand.
4. Arrange the wakame into a serving bowl and pour over the sauce. Garnish with the cucumber, daikon sprouts and lemon wedges.

RICE

I t was not until the late 19th century that the average Japanese could hope to eat rice regularly. Prior to that, the poorer classes (i.e., most of the population) subsisted on cheaper grains such as millet and barley. Although rice plays a lesser role in the izakaya meal as opposed to other Japanese cooking styles, it remains essential to such dishes as *o-chazuke*, *onigiri* rice balls, hotpots, and as a finale to a meal, usually eaten with pickles and *miso* soup. There is only one type of rice used in Japanese cuisine: the short-grained, moist *Japonica* variety, sometimes sold in the West as "sushi rice."

For cooking rice, electric rice cookers do a decent job, but it is hard to beat the depth of aroma and texture you can achieve in a simple *donabe* clay pot, or heavy-lidded saucepan. To make about 3 cups of cooked rice: Rinse 1½ cups of rice, changing the water until it runs almost clear. Strain through a sieve and leave at room temperature for 15 minutes, to allow the rice surface to absorb some amount of the water.

In a dutch oven or heavy pan (about 2.5 qt/2.4L) add the rice and 1½ cups of water, and leave another 15 minutes. Cover the pot with a tight-fitting lid and bring to a boil over about nine minutes. Normally you will see steam or starch bubbles released between the pot and lid. This is normal; nothing needs to be done. Increase the heat to high for about one minute, to create a convection flow in the pot. Lower the heat and cook for 8 minutes. This will gradually steam the rice to the center of its grain. Increase the heat to high for the last 10 seconds of cooking, to evaporate excess moisture. With the lid tightly covered, leave the rice to settle for 15 minutes.

With a wooden spatula, fold the cooked rice in big chunks from the bottom (don't stir or knead). If not serving immediately, stretch a clean cloth between pot and lid to prevent drops of condensation disturbing the rice.

Simmered *Daikon* Radish with Pork and Miso Sauce

There are as many recipes for this winter comfort dish as there are grandmas in Japan. If you wish, any bitterness in the daikon can be softened by simmering in the cloudy water left after rinsing rice. *Recipe p. 20*

The *aji* horse mackerel couldn't come any fresher. The aquarium is situated behind the seating counter, though you might not realize this. Due to the lack of space, Ando has turned this end of the counter into a crockery-and-liquor storage area.

Deep-fried Stuffed Peppers

You can make these delicious morsels—a variation on tempura—more juicy with the addition of minced onion. Note that Japanese *piman* peppers are smaller and thinner skinned than their Western counterparts, so cooking time may vary. *Recipe p. 20*

Simmered *Daikon* Radish with Pork and Miso Sauce

ふろふき大根　肉味噌がけ

Furofuki Daikon, Nikumiso-gake

SERVES 4　　　　　　　　　　　　　　P. 18

Four 1¼ in. (3cm) thick daikon radish rounds, peeled
Strip of *kombu* kelp, 3½ in. (9cm) square
Leftover water from rinsing rice, optional

Sauce

8 oz. (230g) ground pork	1 tbsp. granulated sugar
1 tbsp. finely chopped onion	1 tbsp. soy sauce
	4 tbsp. yellow miso
2 tsp. toasted sesame oil	1 tsp. ketchup

1 tbsp. thinly sliced scallions
1 tsp. minced *yuzu* citrus or lemon peel
Daikon radish sprouts (*kaiware*)

1. For the sauce: Sauté the pork and onions in the oil over medium heat. When the meat is broken up and slightly browned, add sugar, soy sauce, miso, and ketchup. Add water to achieve the consistency of a thick, slightly runny paste. Reduce heat to low and cook, stirring constantly, until smooth (about 5 minutes). Set aside.
2. Bevel top and bottom edges of the daikon rounds and cut a crisscross into one side so that the rounds will keep shape and soften evenly as simmered (you may wish to sculpt the daikon rounds into shapes such as cherry blossoms, as shown).
3. Put the daikon in a medium saucepan and cover completely with cold water, or leftover rice-rinsing water. Gently simmer for 20 minutes, preferably with a drop-lid (glossary p. 153). Drain and rinse under cold water.
4. Put the kombu in the pan and place the daikon (cut side down) onto it. Add water to cover the daikon and bring to a boil. Lower heat and gently simmer until translucent and soft, about 2 hours (add more water as necessary).
5. Arrange daikon on a serving dish, or individual dishes, and ladle the sauce on top. Garnish with the scallions, daikon radish sprouts and yuzu peel. This dish can be served hot or at room temperature.

Deep-fried Stuffed Peppers

ピーマンの肉詰め揚げ

Piman no Niku-zume Age

SERVES 2　　　　　　　　　　　　　　P. 19

1 small green bell pepper (or 2 *piman* peppers)
4½ oz. (125g) ground chicken

Flour for dusting
Vegetable oil for deep frying
Scallions, thinly sliced

Batter

1 cup (4 oz./125g) cake flour
1 cup (240ml) ice cold water

Daikon and Red Chili Relish (*momiji-oroshi*)

½ in. (1.25cm) thick daikon radish round
½ lengths dried red chili pepper.

Tempura Sauce (*tentsuyu*)

¾ (180ml) cup dashi stock　*recipe p. 101
3 tbsp. soy sauce
3 tbsp. mirin
½ cup (120ml) lightly packed dried bonito flakes (*katsuo kezuri-bushi*)
Pinch of salt

1. For the tempura sauce: Bring mirin, soy sauce and dashi just to a boil and turn off heat. Add bonito flakes and leave for 10 seconds, then strain through a fine sieve.
2. For the relish: If the chili is very dry, soak in water for 2 minutes. Cut off the top and remove seeds. Peel and slice the daikon radish into 2 half moons. Sandwich the chili pepper with the daikon segments and finely grate. Alternatively, mix ground chili pepper flakes or shichimi pepper powder with grated daikon radish. If the mash is too watery, drain through a fine sieve.
3. Slice off the top of the green pepper, cut in half lengthwise, and remove seeds and ribs. Lightly dust flour inside and stuff each half with the ground chicken. Dust only the chicken side with flour.
4. In a heavy saucepan, heat 3 in. (7.5cm) of oil to 375°F (190°C). In a medium bowl loosely mix the flour and ice-cold water. The batter should be under-mixed and look lumpy. Coat the green pepper halves with the batter and deep fry in batches until the batter is crisp and golden. To eat: Garnish with the relish and dip in the tempura sauce.

Deep-fried Tofu in Tempura Sauce

揚げだし豆腐
Agedashi-dofu

SERVES 4

P. 22

1 block firm tofu, about 12½ oz. (350g)
Potato starch for coating the tofu
Vegetable oil for frying
Tempura sauce (*tentsuyu*), warm *recipe p. 20
Scallions, thinly sliced
Thin strips of *nori* seaweed (*kizami-nori)*
Daikon and red chili relish (*momiji-oroshi*) *recipe p. 20

1. In a heavy saucepan, heat 2 in. (5cm) of the oil to 360°F (180°C).
2. Slice the tofu into 8 pieces, blot dry and coat with potato starch. Fry the tofu pieces until the surface is golden and crispy, about 5 minutes. When done, the oil will stop bubbling. With a spider strainer or slotted spoon, transfer the tofu onto a paper-lined plate to drain excess oil.
3. Place the tofu in a serving bowl and pour in some tempura sauce. Garnish with the scallions, nori and relish.

RIGHT: Sharing is caring. As the evening picks up pace, customers shout orders as they please. Bills are commonly split, particularly among young people, though office groups are often looked after by the senior member.
TOP: Disposable chopsticks come in individual paper sleeves.

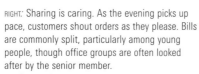

Deep-fried Tofu in Tempura Sauce

Another classic, homestyle pub dish that is a textural sensation, combining the crisp chewiness of the tofu's fried crust with its meltingly soft, creamy insides, all enveloped in delicate tempura dipping sauce. *Recipe p. 21*

Shochu's popularity has far outpaced that of *sake* rice brew. In the foreground, Enma, a limited edition of aged *mugi* (barley) shochu from Oita, on the southern island of Kyushu. The name means "Hell's Gatekeeper."

Julienned Potatoes with Spicy Cod Roe

A Horoyoi original that is one of my all-time favorites. The potatoes should remain crunchy when they arrive on their sizzling platter. Guests can enjoy mixing the cod roe so that it coats the potatoes and cooks through from the residual heat. *Recipe p. 24*

Japanese-style German Potatoes

How this unorthodox style of *Bratkartoffeln* potatoes first appeared on izakaya menus is anyone's guess, but versions like this, in which the potatoes are deep fried and seasoned with soy sauce, have been adored across Japan for generations.   *Recipe p. 24*

Edamame soybeans on the branch. A summer special and, dusted with salt, the ultimate beer snack.

Julienned Potatoes with Spicy Cod Roe

じゃがいもの明太子和え

Jagaimo Mentaiko-ae

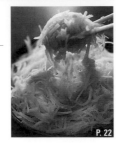

P. 22

SERVES 4

4 medium russet potatoes, peeled
2 tbsp. spicy cod roe (*mentaiko*)
1½ tbsp. vegetable oil
4 pieces unsalted butter, about 1 tsp. each
Salt and freshly ground black pepper

1. With a sharp knife, cut open the membrane sac of the cod roe and carefully scrape out the eggs with the back of the blade or a teaspoon.
2. Peel and finely julienne potatoes. Plunge in cold water to remove excess starch. Drain and dry well.
3. In a large nonstick sauté pan over high heat, heat the oil until hot. Quickly fry the potatoes stirring frequently until slightly softened yet al dente, about 2 minutes. They should not brown. Season with salt and pepper to taste.
4. Immediately arrange potatoes on a sizzling iron platter or a serving bowl. Place the butter and cod roe on top. Mix the cod roe through the potatoes before eating.

Japanese-style German Potatoes

ジャーマン ポテト

Jyaaman Poteto

P. 23

SERVES 2

2 medium russet potatoes
Vegetable oil for deep frying
½ medium onion, sliced ⅛ in. (3mm) thick
1 tsp. vegetable oil
2 strips thick bacon, cut into 1 in. (2.5cm) pieces
½ tsp. soy sauce
1 tbsp. unsalted butter
Salt and freshly ground black pepper
Red leaf lettuce, optional

1. Peel the potatoes and cut into sticks, ½ in. across and 2 in. long (1.25×1.25×5cm). As you cut, plunge them in cold water to prevent browning and to remove excess starch. Drain and pat dry.
2. In a large heavy pan, heat the oil to 325°F (160°C). Fry the potatoes, stirring occasionally until they begin to turn golden, about 5–6 minutes. Increase the heat to 375°F (190°C) and fry until nicely browned, about 2–3 minutes.
3. While deep frying the potatoes, heat 1 tsp. of oil in a large sauté pan over medium high heat and sauté the onion for 4 minutes. Using a spider strainer or slotted spoon, transfer the potatoes into the saute pan. Turn up heat to high, add the bacon and cook until the bacon is lightly cooked.
5. Season with the soy sauce, butter, salt and black pepper. Serve on a bed of lettuce leaves.

Cedar strips at Horoyoi show a few of
the evening's recommendations. When
items run out the strips are taken down.
From the left: a selection of *shochu*
liquors: *ume*, Western plum, apricot,
carrot, and kumquat; salt-grilled fish
head and deep-fried gingko nuts.

Pork and Vegetable Stew

Despite having one of the world's leanest cuisines, the Japanese also love thick pork belly, whether grilled, steamed or boiled. This dish balances nutrition and calories, using plenty of vegetables, *kombu* dashi stock and the curiously textured *konnyaku*. *Recipe p. 28*

Foil-baked Mushrooms

One of the easiest ways to cook mushrooms brimming with natural flavor. Substitute any variety or mixture of mushrooms you like. The lemon is essential, but use only a couple of minutely thin, small slivers. *Recipe p. 28*

Konnyaku: a jelly made from the flour of the "devil's tongue" plant, often confused with a yam. It is high in fiber, low in calories and has almost no taste—but is loved for its texture in *nimono* stews, grilled with *miso* on skewers, or made into noodles to eat with *sukiyaki*. It is commonly avilable flecked with *hijiki* seaweed, which marginally boosts its flavor. Buy it in plastic packs.

Horoyoi-style Rice in Dashi

There's nothing dainty about *o-chazuke* at
the end of an izakaya session. The bowl is
simply lifted to the mouth and the steaming
rice broth shoveled in. It is often prepared
in the home with leftover rice and green
tea instead of dashi. Toppings range from
umeboshi pickled plum to flaked salmon to
wakame. This is a slightly luxurious version.
Recipe p. 29

Pork and Vegetable Stew

豚と野菜の煮込み

Buta to Yasai no Nikomi

SERVES 6–8

½ lb. (230g) fresh pork belly, cut into ½ in. (1.25cm) cubes
1 lb. (450g) *daikon* radish, peeled and cut into ½ in. (1.25cm) cubes
½ lb. (230g) *konnyaku*, cut into ½ in. (1.25cm) cubes
1 medium carrot, peeled and cut into ½ in. (1.25cm) cubes

A ⎡ 1 qt. (1L) or more *kombu dashi* stock recipe below
⎢ 1 tbsp. sugar
⎢ 2 tbsp. soy sauce
⎣ 1 garlic clove, crushed

3 tbsp. yellow miso
Shichimi spice powder (p. 69)
Scallions, for garnish

1. Add water and pork to a medium saucepan, bring to a boil then simmer for 15 minutes. Drain and quickly rinse the pork under running water.
2. Return the pork to the pan, add konnyaku, daikon, carrot and **A**, then bring to a boil. Lower heat, simmer until all ingredients are fork tender, about 3 hours. Add some kombu dashi occasionally so that the ingredients are always covered by liquid. Dissolve miso into the pan and simmer for another 10 minutes. Do not allow to boil, as this will kill the flavor and healthy enzymes of the miso.
3. Ladle the stew into serving bowls. Sprinkle with the scallions and shichimi spice powder.

Kombu *Dashi* stock

MAKES 2 quarts

2 pieces dried *kombu* kelp, 5 in. (12.5cm) square each
2 qt. (2L) cold water

In a 3–4 qt. (3–4L) stock pot, add the kombu and water and let stand at room temperature overnight or for at least 8 hours. Then remove the kombu. If you do not have enough time for this, first soak the kombu for a few hours, then heat the pot over low heat. Remove and discard the kombu as the water begins to simmer, and turn off heat.

Foil-baked Mushrooms

しめじホイル焼き

Shimeji Hoiru-yaki

SERVES 2

1 lb. (450g) *shimeji* mushrooms, trimmed
2 tbsp. unsalted butter, cut into pieces
2 paper-thin of lemon peels, about little-fingernail size
Salt
Soy sauce

1. Make 2 sheets of foil about 12×10 in. (30×25cm).
2. In a bowl, sprinkle salt onto mushrooms. Place the mushrooms in the center of each foil sheet along with the butter and the lemon slice. Make packets by folding up foil sides and then double-folding the tops, leaving room for heat circulation inside.
3. Grill over a low flame for 10–15 minutes until the packet is plump.
4. Put the packets on serving plates, and cut a slit in the top of the foil with a sharp knife, being careful of the released steam. A dash of soy sauce at serving time makes this dish extra delicious.

Horoyoi-style Rice in Dashi

ほろ酔い茶漬け

Horoyoi Chazuke

P. 27

`SERVES` 2

Thin sashimi slices, sushi
  grade
2 cups cooked short-grain
  rice *recipe p. 17
Dashi stock, hot *recipe
  p. 101
Soy sauce

1 sheet of *nori*, crumbled
1 tsp. black sesame seeds,
  toasted
A dab of grated wasabi
A few *mitsuba* leaves to garnish (p. 69.)

Season the dashi stock with soy sauce to a lightly salty
taste and keep hot. If you use squid, diagonally cross-
score the outer skin at ⅛ in. (3mm) intervals with a sharp
knife. Fill individual serving bowls with the cooked rice.
If the rice is cold, reheat by steaming or microwaving.
Arrange the sashimi slices on top of the rice and add the
hot dashi so that it barely covers the sashimi. Top with the
nori, black sesame seeds and mitsuba leaves. Add a dab
of wasabi to the edge of bowl. When eating, dissolve the
wasabi into the broth.

LAST DRINKS FOR GIDGET

It has been lamented by some and hailed by others,
but however you look at it, the passing of Japan's
mizugi — bikini-clad — "beer campaign" girl is a final
reality. In what became a unanimous move beginning
around 2003, the nation's major breweries decided to
phase out their ubiquitous, bouncy beach babes who for
decades dominated izakaya walls with their summery
smiles and impossibly large, frothing mugs. The beauty
contest-like process of choosing the models, and the
media fanfare at their annual announcement, are also
defunct.

"We decided that 'bikini-girl=beer' was rather old-
fashioned," a spokeswoman for Asahi Breweries told
us. "Especially since increasing numbers of women are
attending izakaya." That's certainly true, but whether the
enigmatically smiling, kimono-clad ladies who these days
promote beer are any less objectified (or any more effec-
tive), I have to wonder.

MASTER CLASS

Maru

In Japan, as a rule, the aged get respect, so the longer an izakaya operates the more highly regarded it becomes, regardless of its gourmet credentials. What's odd is that in terms of their premises, such hallowed establishments—especially in Tokyo—are not really old at all. So thoroughly have earthquakes, fires, wartime devastation, and the zeal of developers reconfigured the city that most "legendary" izakaya date back little more than a century. Many have been rebuilt at least once.

Still, with their selling point of history, the old places possess something that the modern izakaya cannot, and the biggest challenge for a new establishment may be how to create an atmosphere that will last. Tokyo is littered with what you could only call failures—those designer izakaya with stunted seating-booths in which you hit your head, or indoor rock gardens dotted with UFO-like sculptures amid horror-movie lighting—many of them relics of Japan's 1980s "bubble" economy. Certainly there are some beautiful modern izakaya, but there are also a disturbing number that seem built to a marketing plan, rather than from any deep love of serving food and drink. Rarely will you find luxurious décor equalled by a seriously good menu.

Enter Maru. Located, perhaps ironically, in the heart of Tokyo's fashion district of

Aoyama, this is indeed a designer izakaya, but it is also a remarkable contemporary establishment where the standard of comfort and food are on an absolutely equal, and very high, level. Maru is the complete package.

Put this down to owner-chef Keiji Mori, his years of experience in a Kyoto *kaiseki* haute cuisine kitchen, his hard-won individualism, and the passion he has instilled in his staff. On a first visit, you may feel there are too many of these bustling young men and women behind the counter, in the kitchen, and working the floor. But see how attentive they are to customer requests (shouted, if you like, in the usual izakaya way, prefaced by a loud "*Sui-ma-sen!*" Excuse me); note their self-confidence and how each is entirely conversant with whatever they are serving; taste the quality of the painstakingly prepared food; and you will conclude that they number just enough. "I don't think of staffing from a business viewpoint," Mori tells me. "That makes you lose focus on what you can give to the customer. And the staff that we have—they work with 120 percent motivation." To maintain this commitment, he takes them on a yearly retreat to a seaside hotel in Chiba. "To discuss what kind of restaurant we are making, and how to change it for the better," he says.

SOME OF MY FRIENDS suggest that Maru is not strictly an izakaya, so superior is its food and setting. But neither is it a typical upmarket Japanese restaurant. The noise level from happy customers on a busy night reaches a steady buzz, and the menu, though of top class ingredients often treated with complex technique, is unpretentious, composed predominantly of small dishes to be shared, and

listed in typical izakaya format, from Char Broiled Dishes to Deep Fried Dishes, Vegetable Dishes, Sashimi, Rice and Noodle Dishes, and with some rarely seen categories, such as "Kyoto Taste" Dishes.

Then there is the room, which despite its understated sophistication, diffused lighting, and chic furniture, is relaxing and practical: you can sit at the counter running the length of the space, interacting with the staff in the slightly sunken preparation area in front of you, or alternatively at one of the generously spaced, heavy timber tables directly opposite, behind which runs a single, comfortable banquette. Although here you are slightly removed from the action, you still feel in touch with it. Had Mori and his designer, Kanmei Yano, been less appreciative of izakaya aesthetics, they might have opted for a much wider "restaurant style" space with more tables, as Maru's floor area is much bigger than it seems (the banquette fronts a false wall behind which lie three small, private dining rooms). But by maintaining this crucial intimacy, Mori and Yano achieved something special, and Maru customers respond by packing the place almost every night.

The final factor in Maru's "izakaya-ness" is that I know Mori's heart is close to the authentic cultural form. On one evening out, sampling down-market pubs in Tokyo's suburbs, we ate skewers of *han-yaki* (half-raw) organ meats at a foldup table in a hole-in-the-wall establishment and drank the local drink, black *Hoppy* non-alcohol beer mixed with shots of semifrozen *shochu*. I could see on Mori's face a palpable enjoyment at stepping into these worlds, contemplating the menus—universes removed from his own—and how they related to local wants.

The word "*maru*" most commonly means "circle," and Mori's understanding of this, though he has chosen an arcane Chinese character to express it, is *to circulate happiness*. "First, through our own pleasure—from cooking," he says. "Because if we don't have this, we can't pass on anything."

He once lost this enjoyment. After developing his cooking skills at the izakaya owned by his mother, he started working in the early 1980s as a pot-washer at Isecho, one of Kyoto's most venerated *ryotei* kaiseki restaurants, where he rose to the position of *ni-kata*, or chef in charge of *dashi* soups and simmering stocks. These are the cornerstones of a Japanese restaurant's signature taste. "The *nimono* [simmered foods] really demonstrate a restaurant's level," says Mori. "And if the ni-kata changes, regular patrons will know." Even after achieving this rank, it takes several years to be confident enough with the timing and seasoning to produce a consistent taste for the head chef. After seven years, Mori thinks he nailed it. "I got the skill from my chef on a one-to-one basis, which was truly precious to me," he says.

But the strict hierarchy of ryotei culture frustrated him. "There are many good points about apprenticing in a traditional Kyoto kitchen, but also some bad," he says. "The people above you are always right—regardless. If they say white is black, you have no choice but to go along with them. I found it tedious."

So in 1987, he quit Isecho, cooked at various other restaurants, worked on perfecting his English, and several years later enrolled in a business course at a college in California. More than his studies, his new environment delivered an epiphany. "The other students were constantly talking about their dreams, and everyone was different—there was an accountant, a doctor, the founder of a company—and I realized that to be a cook was not the only way," he says. "I felt I could become anything, and once I'd reached this neutral frame of mind, I understood that I loved making food, and then I knew that I could freely go back to cooking."

CUTTING SHORT his studies, he returned to Tokyo, energized and—in his words—more empowered than any fifteen- or eighteen-year-old working in a Kyoto ryotei, cooking because they "had to." While the seeds of his dream grew, he ran his mother's izakaya, then took on a chain-store café franchise, and in 2001 opened Maru in Azabu Juban in central Tokyo. Within a few years he had a solid clientele, but renovations by the building owner forced him to move. "We really didn't want to," says Mori, but his customers came with him, including a growing base of Westerners, whose appreciation of Maru is reciprocated with Mori's provision of that rarest of izakaya commodities: an English-language menu.

Mori is a maverick in the izakaya world: whereas many izakaya will be nervous about greeting non-Japanese customers, fearing the mutual lack of language will lead to dissatisfaction, he is on a mission to disseminate Japanese cuisine, or *washoku*. For Mori, the more foreign customers the better, and this is not merely a business stance. His time in the US infused him with an enthusiasm for all food; he is an internationalist and a certified sommelier whose izakaya maintains an extensive wine list. In 2006 Mori joined a small group of food professionals on a tour of the Napa Valley, and cooked in his rented accommodation for guests who included top

Green Beans with Sesame Sauce

Sweet and nutty sesame sauce is a simple, traditional Japanese accompaniment to vegetables in season. Enjoy experimenting with other cooking greens such as spinach, broccoli rabe, turnip leaves, Swiss chard or mustard greens.   *Recipe p. 36*

US chefs and graduates from the Culinary Institute of America. Some of them arrived hours early, eager to help in the kitchen.

"The great point about washoku is that you can share so many small dishes," he says. "We use so many vegetables, beans and seaweeds, it's absolutely healthy." The quality of these ingredients comes at a premium, and Maru is not cheap. But considering you receive kaiseki quality and the izakaya freedom to construct a meal at your leisure, it is genuine value for money. "Ryotei take almost too much care," Mori says. "They excessively greet customers, make great interiors and gardens, and offer huge hospitality. But all this demands big budgets. I want to tell people that washoku can be delicious without extravagant ingredients. We often serve very good beef at Maru, but items like this are not 'on parade.' This is my restaurant."

Steamed and Grilled Pork with Salt

The double cooking technique of this dish renders most of the fat from the pork, but leaves a delicious, meaty roundness of flavor. A good dish for the barbecue. Cook at a distance from medium-hot coals, to allow infrared heat to penetrate.   *Recipe p. 37*

Green Beans with Sesame Sauce

いんげんの胡麻和え
Ingen no Goma-ae

P. 34

SERVES 4

7 oz. (200g) green beans
1 oz. (30g) deep-fried tofu pouch (*abura-age*), optional
8–12 shucked fava beans, optional

Toasted white sesame seeds, optional
All-purpose *dashi* stock *recipe below
Salt

White Sesame Sauce
2 oz. (60g) white sesame seeds, ¼ cup, toasted
  * Substitute with tahini as desired. See method in Step 1.
1 tbsp. granulated sugar
1 tbsp. soy sauce
3 tbsp. *sake*

1. For the sesame sauce: In a small frying pan over low heat, toast the sesame seeds until fragrant, taking care not to burn them. Pulse in a food processor to your preferred consistency—either smooth or a little coarse. (The ideal tool for this job, if you have one, is a *suribachi* mortar—see glossary p. 155. The mortar gives a mashed paste, moist with the seeds' oil, whereas the food processor tends to cut the seed fibers.) Transfer the paste to a bowl and add the sugar, soy sauce and sake. Mix, scraping down the side of the bowl with a rubber spatula. Adjust the consistency with dashi stock or sake to the equivalent of a loose peanut butter. If you wish to skip the preceding steps, simply combine some tahini with the sugar, soy sauce and sake.

2. Trim both ends of the green beans and cut into 1¼ in. (3cm) pieces. Have ice water ready in a medium bowl. Bring a large pot of salted water to boil and cook the green beans until crisp-tender, about 10 minutes. Using a spider strainer, transfer the beans into the ice water, shock and drain. Soak in the all-purpose dashi stock (*happo dashi*—see below) in a medium bowl for 1 hour.

3. Cook the fava beans in the same large pot with salted boiling water until tender, about 3 minutes. You don't need to shock them in cold water. Peel off the waxy skins.

4. Cut the deep-fried tofu into strips about ¼ in.(6mm) wide and 1¼ in. (3cm) long. Have boiling water ready in a kettle or small pot. To remove excess oil from the fried tofu, put the strips in a sieve, pour boiling water over them, drain and lightly press in paper towels. Blanch in the all-purpose dashi stock.

5. Lightly squeeze out the excess liquid from the green beans and tofu strips, put them in a large bowl along with the fava beans and mix with the sesame sauce. Arrange in a serving bowl and sprinkle with toasted sesame seeds.

All-purpose *Dashi* Stock (*happo dashi*)

1 qt. (1L) dashi stock *recipe p. 101
¼ cup (60ml) soy sauce
1 tsp. sea salt or to taste

Combine all ingredients in a large bowl or container. Ladle out as needed.

Steamed and Grilled Pork with Salt

蒸し豚の塩焼き
Shiobuta no Mushi-yaki

P. 42

SERVES 4

1 lb. (450g) block of fresh pork belly, rind removed
Sea salt
2 tbsp. grated *daikon* radish
1 tsp. soy sauce
2 scallions, white part, thinly julienned
1 *shiso* leaf, julienned
1 tsp. grated ginger
1–2 tsp. fresh lemon juice
Sprigs of Italian parsley, as garnish

1. Take a large pot fitted with a steamer insert and fill with water to the bottom of the steamer. Bring the water to a boil over high heat, place the pork belly in the steamer, and cover and cook until tender, about 2 hours. Remove the pork belly and set aside at room temperature. When cool enough to handle, cut the pork belly into 4¼ oz. (120g) blocks.
2. Build a rather cool charcoal fire or preheat a gas grill to medium-low. Make about 6–8 in. (15–20cm) space between the fire and grate. Heat the grate for 2 minutes.
3. Thread the pork pieces onto metal skewers and season with salt and pepper. Grill the skewered pork on the grate, taking care not to brown, until the pork fat is rendered and drops off, about 8–10 minutes. Remove the pork from the skewers and cut into bite-size pieces.
4. Season the grated daikon radish with the soy sauce and set aside.
5. Combine the julienned scallion, julienned shiso and grated ginger.
6. Arrange the pork pieces on a serving plate, top with grated daikon radish and the scallion mixture. Sprinkle with lemon juice and garnish with Italian parsley.

Rarely used in the home, steel chopsticks, or *kanabashi*, are indispensable to the chef wishing to make the best presentation. Their sharp tips allow a sensitive touch for arranging food and garnishes. Also shown: a *yanagiba* sashimi knife.

Deep-fried Tilefish

In this unusual dish, the fish is cooked with its
scales on. The scales bloom like flower petals and
have a delightful crispy texture. *Recipe p. 40*

Ripe Tomato and Cucumber Salad

This salad is almost all "crunch," and bursts with goodness in the mouth. Use the sweetest tomatoes you can find. *Recipe p. 40*

O-shinko, or pickles, are a favorite accompaniment to rice and *sake* — indeed, many sake drinkers eat only pickles as they tipple. Shown here are yellow *takuan* daikon, cucumber, eggplant, and, on the right, orange pickled ginger. Maru makes its own pickles daily and serves them with claypot-cooked rice.

Deep-fried Tilefish

甘鯛の花揚げ

Amadai no Hana-age

P. 38

MAKES 10 pieces

One 14 in. (35cm) whole tilefish, 1⅓ lbs. (600g),
   scale and skin intact, or 10½ oz. (300g) fillets in total
Cake flour
5 half *sudachi* citrus rounds or 5 lemon wedges
Oil for deep frying

1. Scrub and rinse the tilefish under running cold water. Do not remove the scales. Pat dry with a paper towel. On a clean cutting board, cut off the head and remove the innards. Thoroughly rinse the blood from the fish and pat dry (be sure to dry well inside the belly). With a sharp fish knife or *deba* knife, cut the fish into fillets and remove the flesh from the backbone. Slice the ribs from the fillets and remove the pin bones with tweezers. Generously sprinkle both sides of each fillet with salt and lay them scale side down on a paper-lined tray. Cover with plastic wrap and refrigerate for 3 hours.
2. In a large heavy saucepan, preheat the oil to 360°F (180°C). Cut the fillets crosswise into 1 oz. (30g) pieces and dust with flour on the flesh side. Deep fry the pieces scale-side-up in small batches. The scales should immediately stand up and begin to bubble. Fry for about 3–4 minutes, turn once and fry until golden, about 1 minute. Transfer to a paper-lined plate to drain any excess oil.
3. Arrange on a serving plate with the citrus.

Ripe Tomato and Cucumber Salad

完熟トマトと叩き胡瓜のサラダ

Kanjuku-tomato to Tataki Kyuri no Salada

P. 39

SERVES 4

Marinade for lotus root
⅓ cup (80ml) water
1 tbsp. rice vinegar
1 tsp. sugar
A pinch of salt

2 small to medium best vine-ripened tomatoes
1 Japanese cucumber or ⅓ English cucumber, unpeeled
⅔ oz. (20g) *renkon* lotus root
¼ medium red onion
4–8 whole snow peapods
2 tsp. white sesame seeds, lightly toasted

Dressing
1 large egg yolk
⅓ cup (80ml) or more
  vegetable oil
Scant ½ cup yellow miso
¼ cup (60ml) *sudachi* citrus
  juice or lemon juice
1 scant tbsp. (12g) soy
  sauce

1. For the marinade: In a small saucepan, combine all marinade ingredients and bring to a boil. Immediately remove from heat and let cool to room temperature. Cut the lotus root into ⅛ in. (3mm) thick rounds and soak in vinegared water for 5 minutes. Briefly blanch in boiling water and soak in the marinade until flavored, for 20 minutes.
2. Slice the red onion into very thin slices. If the onion is bitter, soak in ice-cold water for about 20 minutes to crisp it and remove harshness. Drain well.
3. Have ice water ready in a small bowl. In a small saucepan, bring salted water to a boil and blanch the snow peas for about 2 minutes. Using a spider strainer, transfer the snow peas into the ice water to stop cooking. Drain.
4. Cut the tomato into 6–8 wedges. Lightly pound the cucumber on a cutting board with a rolling pin to soften it and allow the dressing to penetrate, and cut into 1¼ in. (3.5cm) lengths.
5. For the dressing: in a medium bowl, beat egg yolk and gradually add 5 Tbsp. of the vegetable oil, first drop by drop, then in a very thin stream whisking vigorously all the while. The oil should be completely emulsified. If it breaks up, start over with a new egg yolk. Mix in miso, sudachi citrus juice and soy sauce, and adjust thickness by whisking in about 3 tbsp. of the vegetable oil.
6. Pat dry onion and snow peas. Arrange all vegetables on a serving plate. Spoon over the dressing and sprinkle with the sesame seeds.

You do it like this. . . . One of the factors behind Maru's consistent high quality is master Keiji Mori's dedication to training and enthusing his staff.

Even the disposable utensils are chic, and you won't find these in just any izakaya. Hexagonal cross-section chopsticks feel elegant in the hand and are easy to use when gripping the slipperiest of foods.

Deep-fried Fish Cakes

The key to these flavorful fish cakes is the contrast between the oily, blueskin fish and white-fleshed fish. Be aware that minced fish goes off rather quickly, so don't store the raw preparation for too long. If desired, you can deep fry in advance then reheat over a grill.

Recipe p. 44

Foil-baked Potatoes

A touch of Japanese seasoning (soy sauce, *sansho*) transforms this elementary dish into something special. Make sure to use new potatoes.

Recipe p. 44

SASHIMI

There is an excellent reason why *sashimi* is the opening act to almost every izakaya meal: its delicacy is upstaged by the savory dishes that follow. Good sashimi has no fishy taste or odor, only the natural sweetness of the fish you have chosen. The chef will adjust his cutting depending on the variety and part of the fish being used. Here, the *chu toro* semi-fatty tuna belly is presented in bite-sized blocks, so that diners can enjoy a hearty hit of the fish's creamy richness. The *tai* snapper, at bottom, is sliced thin-but-not-too-thin, to make the most of the snapper's lean *al dente* texture. The *ika*, or squid, having a somewhat tough outer layer, is cut into noodle-like strips.

This presentation on crushed ice is more glamorous than most, featuring visual garnishes of cucumber flowers and summer maple leaves, and edible accompaniments of radish, fresh grated *wasabi* and the gelatinous seed *bakudaikai*, which provides more texture than taste. Most izakaya serve sashimi on a bed of shredded *daikon* radish, with a fresh *shiso* leaf, wasabi, and perhaps shiso buds and the red micro vegetable *beni-tade*.

When eating sashimi, pour a small amount of soy sauce into your dish, add some shiso buds and beni-tade (if provided), and either stir in some wasabi or place the wasabi directly on the fish, then lightly dip the combination into the sauce (this is the best way to enjoy fresh wasabi). Any good chef will look aghast at diners who swamp or soak sashimi in lashings of wasabi and soy.

It is not necessarily true that the fresher the fish the better. Many chefs hold that the flesh of just-killed fish is too "tight," and that fish benefits from a day or two's rest, to allow its texture and flavor to deepen. But sashimi should never be soggy or limp, or have stained the daikon it is served on (indicating it has been left sitting). It should never be served semi-frozen, and should not even be especially cold: about halfway between body- and fridge-temperature is about right.

Some variations on sashimi are not raw fish but still extremely popular. These include *kohada*, a vinegared sort of shad, and, in summer, *shime saba*, or lightly pickled mackerel. Both intentionally have a somewhat fishy taste. It is crucial that mackerel, an oily fish that easily turns—particularly in summer—be as fresh as possible.

Deep-fried Fish Cakes

さつま揚げ

Satsuma-age

P. 42

MAKES 12 cakes

1 lb. (450g) *aji* horse mackerel fillets, bone and skin removed
½ lb. (230g) cod or pollock fillets, bone and skin removed
2 oz. (60g) *gobo* burdock root, shaved as if sharpening a
   pencil *see glossary for *sasagaki*
All purpose *dashi* stock (*happo dashi*) *recipe p. 36

Seasonings
⅓ cup (80ml) dashi stock *recipe p. 101
2 tsp. *sake*
1 tbsp. granulated sugar
1½ tsp. soy sauce
1¼ oz. (40g) white miso
Tamamoto (mix 1 large egg yolk and 1 tbsp. vegetable oil
   in a ramekin ahead of time)

Vegetable oil for deep frying
Grated ginger and grated wasabi as condiments
Soy sauce for dipping

1. On a paper-lined sheet pan, lightly salt the mackerel fillets, cover with plastic wrap and refrigerate for 2 hours.
2. In a food processor, pulse and grind the fillets into a coarse paste. Transfer into a bowl and set aside.
3. Blanch the shavings of burdock root in the all purpose dashi stock, drain and set aside.
4. Pulse the cod or pollock in a food processor, gradually adding ⅓ cup of the dashi stock. Add sake, sugar, soy sauce and white miso, then give a few more pulses. Transfer the mixture into a large bowl. Add the aji horse mackerel paste, the egg-oil mixture (tamamoto) and the burdock shavings. Mix well with rubber spatula. Make 12 oval cakes, about ⅔ in. (1.5cm) thick. Lay on a sheet pan lined with parchment paper, cover tightly with plastic wrap and refrigerate for 20 minutes.
5. To deep fry: In a large heavy saucepan, heat the oil to 340°F (170°C). Deep fry the cakes until golden brown, about 4–5 minutes. Transfer to a paper-lined plate to drain excess oil.
6. To serve: Cut each cake into quarters and arrange on a plate with the grated ginger and wasabi on the side. Serve soy sauce in individual small dishes for dipping the cakes.

Foil-baked Potatoes

じゃがいものホイル焼き

Jagaimo no Hoiru-yaki

P. 42

SERVES 2

6 small new potatoes
2 spears asparagus
2 large *shiitake* mushrooms
1 tbsp. unsalted butter
Sea salt
Freshly ground black pepper
1 tsp. soy sauce
1 tbsp. sour cream
A pinch of ground sansho pepper or black pepper
Kinome leaves, as garnish

1. Scrub the potatoes, leaving the skin intact. Steam or boil until easily pierced through with a skewer, about 15–20 minutes. Remove from heat, let cool at room temperature, and remove skin.
2. Cut the tough part from the bottom of each asparagus spear, and peel each spear for about 1 in. (2.5cm) at its bottom. Cut into bite-size-pieces. For the shiitake mushrooms, cut the tough part off the stem and slice into halves.
3. Make a sheet of aluminum foil, 10×14 in. (25.5× 36cm). Place the potatoes, asparagus, shiitake mushrooms, and butter on the center of the sheet. Sprinkle with salt, pepper and soy sauce. Make a packet by bringing up foil sides and tightly double-folding top ends, leaving a little room for heat circulation inside.
4. Heat a griddle or grill over medium-high heat. Place the packets on top and grill until the asparagus and shiitake mushrooms are cooked, about 10–15 minutes (swelling of the packets with steam indicates they are just about cooked).
5. Arrange the packets on a serving plate and cut a crisscross opening. Spoon sour cream on top, sprinkle with sour cream ground sansho pepper or ground black pepper, and garnish with kinome leaves.

At Maru you can take part in traditional "interactive" dining: grilling a selection of dried fish over a portable charcoal brazier. It is both physically and spiritually warming.

Simmered *Kamo*-eggplant and Pork Loin

賀茂なすと豚のやわらか煮

Kamo-nasu to Buta no Yawaraka-ni

SERVES 4

1 lb. (450g) pork loin, cut crosswise into halves
2 tsp. vegetable oil
1 large eggplant (or 2 Japanese eggplants)
1½ cups all-purpose *dashi* stock * recipe p. 36

Simmering Liquid

⌈ 1 qt. (1L) water
  4 tbsp. sugar
  ½ cup (240ml) *sake*
⌊ ¾ cup (180ml) soy sauce

Sauce

⌈ ½ cup (120ml) reserved liquid *see details in Step 2
  ¼ cup (60ml) dashi stock * recipe p. 101
  2 tsp. sake
  1 tsp. soy sauce
  1 tsp. granulated sugar
  1½ tsp. *kudzu* starch or potato starch
⌊ 2 tsp. water

Vegetable oil for deep frying
Chives, thinly sliced
Dijon mustard

1. Heat the vegetable oil in a large frying pan. When smoking hot, add the pork loin and sauté until slightly browned all over.

2. In a pressure cooker, add all ingredients of the simmering liquid together with the pork loin. Following the manufacturer's instructions, attach the lid, lock, and bring to high pressure. Lower heat to maintain pressure and cook for 35 minutes. Turn off the heat and allow to come to normal pressure naturally, about 5–10 minutes. Remove the lid, tilting the cooker away from you. Remove the pork and reserve ½ cup (120ml) of the simmering liquid.

3. Meanwhile, prepare the eggplant. (If using Western cut in half and deseed.) Cut off the tip and score a few lines on the skin to prevent the eggplant from exploding. Heat the oil to 340°F (170°C) and deep fry until soft, about 4 minutes (deep fry Japanese eggplants for 2 minutes). Plunge in water and peel off the skin by hand. Cut in half lengthwise. In a small saucepan, add the all-purpose *dashi* stock and eggplant, bring to a simmer, and remove from heat. Set aside.

4. For the sauce: in a small cup, dissolve the kudzu starch in water. In a medium saucepan, add the liquid reserved from Step 2, dashi stock, sake, soy sauce and sugar. Bring to a boil, lower heat and add the kudzu slurry to thicken the sauce.

5. Cut the pork into bite-sized pieces. Cut the eggplant lengthwise into 2–3 pieces. Arrange in serving bowls and ladle over the thickened sauce. Garnish with the chives and a dab of mustard.

The *kamo-nasu* eggplant from Kyoto is close to the American eggplant in shape but has thinner skin. It is essential to *kaiseki* cooking. It suits simmering, and in combination with meats, produces a rich juice.

Fresh Corn *Kakiage* Tempura

とうもろこしのかき揚げ

Tomorokoshi no Kakiage

MAKES 3 *kakiage*

1 ear of corn, to yield about
1 cup of kernels
1–3 mild chili peppers such
as Amanaga or Anaheim,
skin pierced
Cake flour
Oil for deep frying

Batter
⌈ 1 cup (4 oz./125g) cake
  flour
  1 large egg yolk
⌊ 1 cup (240ml) ice water

Sea salt

1. For the batter: In a small bowl, mix the batter ingredients.
2. Place corn kernels in a medium bowl and sprinkle with a little flour. Spoon the batter into the bowl and lightly combine.
3. Heat the oil to 340°F (170°C). With a serving spoon, scoop up ⅓ of the mixture and carefully slip into the oil and deep fry. Repeat for another two batches. Turn gently a couple of times, until slightly golden and crispy, about 2–3 minutes. Deep fry chili peppers (without batter) until soft. Transfer onto a paper-lined dish to drain excess oil.
4. Arrange on a serving plate and eat with sea salt.

FOUR SEASONS

Advances in farming and distribution, coupled with disruptions to weather patterns, have blurred the line between Japan's seasons. Many fish species are farmed year round, the import trade delivers almost anything at any time, and in southern Japan there are farmers who heat their soil to produce bamboo shoots—a spring delicacy—in mid-winter. Yet there are still dishes eaten only at New Year's, and there remains a single day in summer dedicated to the eating of eels. In short, the Japanese are one of the world's most season-conscious people, and any food in season is said to be in its *shun*. Here are some specialties to look out for on your izakaya visit.

Spring (Mar.–May): Fish and shellfish: early bonito (*hatsu-gatsuo*); red sea bream (*tai*); miniature shrimp (*sakura*); firefly squid (*hotaru ika*); ark shell (*akagai*); cockle (*torigai*). Vegetables: bamboo shoots (*takenoko*); broccoli rabe (*nanohana*).

Summer (June–Aug.): Fish: horse mackerel (*aji*); grunt (*isaki*); sardines (*iwashi*); Japanese sea bass (*suzuki*); flathead (*kochi*); pike eel (*hamo*); sweetfish (*ayu*); sea eel (*anago*); common squid (*surume ika*). Vegetables: tomatoes; water shield (*junsai*); corn; soybeans (*edamame*).

Autumn (Sept.–Nov.): Fish: late bonito (*modori gatsuo*); oysters (*kaki*); Pacific saury (*sanma*); mackerel (*saba*). Vegetables: mushrooms (*matsutake, maitake* etc.); eggplant (*nasu*); lotus root (*renkon*).

Winter (Dec.–Feb.): Fish and shellfish: monkfish (*anko*); cod (*tara*); crab (*kani*); scallops (*hotate*); turtle (*suppon*); yellowtail (*buri*); puffer fish (*fugu*); sea urchin (*uni*). Vegetables: turnips (*kabu*).

IZAKAYA—A POTTED HISTORY

Izakaya have evolved in step with seemingly unrelated upheavals in Japanese society. During the 1980s "bubble economy," for example, when the stock market hit the stratosphere and almost any entrepreneur with a half-baked business plan could find himself eligible for a profligate bank loan, the commercial areas of Tokyo saw the spread of gauche "nouveau izakaya."

The food and décor at these establishments was a vulgar jumble of style over substance, but the "bubble" izakaya had its good points: it popularized izakaya culture among a new, cashed-up generation that wanted to share food and drink in convivial surroundings.

Crucially, this group included large numbers of women, who had previously been marginalized by izakaya culture. When the economy collapsed in 1990 and consumers became more realistic about their spending, these new izakaya customers, seeking a more authentic experience, focused their outings on older establishments. Thus the post-bubble generation re-energized the old izakaya, many of which are today as busy as they have ever been.

The 20th century remains well represented by Tokyo's izakaya, with establishments such as Mimasuya in Kanda, which began business in 1905. Kagiya, in Negishi, which opened its doors as a liquor store in 1856, started to allow drinking on its premises in 1925, and began serving food in 1949. In Jujo, in Tokyo's far northwest, the classic one-room *taishu sakaba*, or "people's drinking store," Saito Sakaba, also had its roots as a liquor retailer, but was forced to shut its doors when most of its menfolk—who lugged the heavy sake barrels—were lost to the war. The women who remained converted the store to an izakaya, and bustling "aunties," or *obasan*, of a disarming cheerfulness continue to operate Saito Sakaba today.

There are numerous other examples, but if the above suggests that izakaya evolved only from liquor stores, this was not the case. Commoners could not freely drink alcohol until the Edo period (1603–1867), though the number of instances in which the authorities decreed a prohibition on sake, from the Heian period (794–1185) onward, indicates how difficult this was to enforce.

Records suggest that noodle vendors and innkeepers established some kind of precursor to the izakaya, serving food and drink in a relaxed setting. But it was in the Edo period that izakaya began taking the shape we know today—most likely through the restaurant-like establishments, or *niuriya*, that sold simmered foods in broth, then later *sashimi*, *tempura* and other fish and vegetable dishes (meat being against Buddhist precepts).

Despite government efforts to ban the more licentious of these stores, which were sometimes fronts for brothels, the niuriya were vital to the city of Edo (now

Edo-period izakaya. Note the lack of chairs, the hanging fish and poultry, and sake being drunk from large pots, or *chirori*, by an exclusively male clientele. Today, the laughter and feasting may be unchanged, but the participation of women is certainly welcome progress.

Muda Shugyo Kane no Waraji/Juppensha Ikku/National Diet Library

European-style "beer halls" were the places to be at the end of the Meiji period, and Japan's major breweries continue to operate them. Here, the disorderly izakaya patrons (inset) sit cramped onto small sake barrels, as formally dressed beer drinkers are clearly more "civilized."

Tokyo Fuzokushi/Hirade Kenjiro/National Diet Library

Tokyo), especially at such times as the massive Meireki Fire of 1657, which destroyed some two-thirds of the city.

The enormous task of rebuilding generated a huge influx of laborers and artisans, who naturally wanted pub-like places where they could unwind, and this most likely sparked the first izakaya "boom." Ironically, other periods of enlivened izakaya activity also pivoted on disasters, such as the period following the Great Kanto Earthquake of 1923, and of course World War II. Bars and eating places sprang up simply because citizens had nowhere else to go.

Izakaya further evolved with the Westernization ushered in by the Meiji period (1868–1912), when the eating of meat such as *yakitori* (grilled chicken) and *yakiton* (grilled pork) became popular. The era also saw the advent of the "beer hall," modeled on the German pub, though Japan's first Western-influenced izakaya was most likely the Kamiya Bar in Asakusa, dating from 1880. Extensively renovated, the Kamiya does a huge trade over three floors, and continues serving its own firewater liquor, Denki Bran (literally, electric brandy), a mix of cheap liqueurs and flavoring agents, which you drink at your own risk!

More recently, the 1960s saw the izakaya influenced by the food-service model of the American hamburger chain, and dozens of corporations now operate thousands of franchise izakaya throughout Japan. Most of them have uniform décor and "branding," along with laminated plastic menus showing photographs of dishes, and wait-staff armed with Palm Pilot-like wireless ordering gadgets.

Establishment unknown, 1955. The mistress (*o-kamisan*) is heating sake flasks. Menu notices around the room include items such as "Cheese: 20 yen," "Meat stew: 20 yen," and "Large beer: 130 yen."

Photo: Kyodo News

It is unfortunate that the word "izakaya," for many young people of drinking age, conjures only such chain stores. But there are reasons for optimism: thanks to the spread of social networking and blogging, it has become something of a brag to be able to recount knowledge of Tokyo's most authentic, inexpensive, classic, and sometimes obscure establishments.

The only doubt is that the masters or madams of many of these older establishments have no ensuing generation willing or able to continue the tradition. Today's chain-izakaya-goers may eventually catch on to the deep and evocative pleasures of the individual pub. Hopefully, they will make it in time.

DREAM ON

 Saiki

One early summer evening with the unaccustomed humidity making me sweat, I set off alone for Saiki. Though I have no appointment to keep I am later than I want to be, so I hurry, consoled to some degree in knowing that if it's best to arrive early, it also helps to go alone. Only a dozen customers can fit at Saiki's counter, four each at its two tiny tables, and though there is a small upstairs area for groups, the place fills up almost instantly.

Kunihiko Saiki and his self-named establishment are a Tokyo institution, and if you spend a little time here you will see that it is not only non-Japanese who feel daunted at brushing through an unfamiliar izakaya's *noren* entrance curtain. Watch how apologetically the first-time customer slides open the fragile door and pokes his head in, peering around like a lost animal and nodding shyly to one of the three stern female waitresses. He raises his fingers to show how many are in his group. If invited to enter they will take their seats with a quick, dipping bow to the master, who, when he is not in the kitchen, will be overseeing his domain from the front of the room, tucked behind the narrow corner of the L-shaped counter, dressed in a crisp white chef's smock, only inches from his customers.

Known to regulars as Kuni-san, the master is quick with a joke and effuses an insouciant, masculine recklessness typical of the working-class man-about-town—he has what the Japanese call "*iki*." Saiki has no admission policy, but whether it's simply the atmosphere, or word of mouth, or press reports, patrons sense that a certain deportment is expected. In short, Saiki has an aura. It also has the credentials to back this up.

Opened in 1948 by Sakurako Saiki, Kuni's mother, from the early 1950s the pub became a regular haunt of several major figures in Japan's "Third Generation" of post war literati. Upstairs, in 1953, when an intellectual magazine hosted a round-table discussion on contemporary literature, the chairman of the talk was Shusaku Endo, described by Graham Greene as one of the twentieth century's finest authors. Other participants included at least three soon-to-be winners of the prestigious Akutagawa Prize. Mind you, this was no polite, tea-sipping book circle, but a hotheaded debate over a radical new literature that would confront themes such as post-war malaise, alienation, sexual deviance, and madness, among others.

The more extreme of those who became Saiki regulars included Yoshiyuki Junnosuke, an inveterate gambler, brothel-frequenter, and Akutagawa winner whose exploits are reflected in his novels. And there was the troubled critic who made a point of paying his respects to Madame Saiki before disappearing into the mountains to kill himself. Also dropping by was Toshio Shimao, whose time as a naval suicide squad cadet (the war finished before he could be utilized) forms the basis of several of his books, and whose calligraphy is displayed upstairs: the single character, *Dream*.

But this was in the past. Kuni plays it down, insisting that the writers who gathered at Saiki when he was a child were not famous at the time. "And it's not as if we had so many splendid patrons then, and now we don't," he tells me. "We have many excellent customers these days." Indeed, some have been regulars for forty years and as a result treat him somewhat like a mischievous boy, ribbing him mercilessly, which he takes wryly in stride.

SAIKI'S CULTURAL channeling is ongoing, and when the izakaya closes its doors for the weekend, Kuni regularly turns it into a kind of salon. Here I attended a performance of *rakugo*, or traditional comic story telling, in the same upstairs room as that long-ago literary debate, crowded onto thin cushions upon the reed mat floor with seventeen others, while for the next hour, on a red cloth-covered dais in front of us, the raconteur sat on his haunches and, with only a folding fan as a prop, delivered his energetic tales. Afterward, when the applause had subsided, Kuni directed us downstairs, where we filled all available stools for the evening's second act. Several of the regulars had donated large *issho-bin* bottles of special regional *sake* and Kuni and his staff provided a simmered squid appetizer. Drinking and talking over the next two hours, I felt I made new friends, and if we shared little in common apart from an appreciation of the moment, and of Saiki, it was a precious izakaya experience.

Sakurako Saiki would not allow Kuni-san to work in the izakaya as a child, and he learned to cook as a young adult at two other restaurants which she owned, only returning to take charge before she passed away in 1999. Saiki is highly regarded for its menu, which is small and seasonal, and Kuni upholds his mother's taste and techniques, though he has sourced his own recipes widely, from friends and sometimes other establishments—such as the superb crab cream croquettes that come from a legendary Western-style Japanese restaurant. He warns that with any recipe the cook must account for the varying size, thickness, and oil content of different pieces of fish, not just between species, but between seasons. A *saba* mackerel in autumn, for example, when it is full of juicy fat, is a far superior *sashimi* fish to one caught in summer, when the best use for it is to vinegar it for pickled *shime saba*.

Kuni's approach to food is no-nonsense, expressed in his belief that in an ideal world cooking would not, in fact, be necessary. "The best food is best eaten raw," he says. "The only reason we have chefs is because ingredients decay, and once something has lost its freshness, we fry and steam and so on." Ironically, the deep-fried food at Saiki is excellent, though Kuni scoffs when I ask his secret. "There's nothing to it," he insists. Why, then, are so many poor deep-fried dishes served elsewhere? "It all comes down to the oil," he says. "And temperature. You have to turn up the heat at the end of frying, to make the oil drain well from the food. And use good oil and change it often. There's nothing else. Anyway," he adds, with endearing dismissiveness, "it's not as if fish for frying is really any good."

IT IS 6:30 P.M. and still daylight when I arrive. To let in the breeze, Kuni has left the door open, and the flowering shrubs flanking each side of it—gardenia and a multi-hued jasmine—are thick with fragrance. Peering in through the doorway I see a space at the counter and am directed to sit there by a waitress, squeezing in gratefully alongside three elderly regulars who I recognize. We exchange nods and they carry on their intimate banter—all but impenetrable to me, having just arrived—peppered with puns and quotes from poems.

A waitress brings the *otoshi* appetizers—not one perfunctory dish but three, for which every diner pays about triple the average izakaya charge. But it is a small price for entry, and depending on how long you stay, you are not necessarily obliged to order more. I receive in a small cup-like dish a preparation of fresh *mekabu* seaweed in vinegar, seasoned with slivers of fresh ginger; steamed segments of asparagus in black sesame dressing; and *aji-su* vinegared horse mackerel with grated ginger and soy sauce to dip. The collection's astringent coolness gives it a summery feel, and I order *shochu* "*rokku*" (on the rocks) with a lemon wedge to accompany it. I might have chosen instead the Saiki special: *toketsu-shu*, or semi-frozen sake. This snow-like slurry of generic rice brew is shaken into your glass from a bottle kept in the freezer. As you drink off the liquid you will soon realize it packs a considerable punch. "The liquid is concentrated alcohol, since it doesn't freeze," says Kuni, and tonight I take the wiser route and avoid it.

The tenor of the group changes when another regular, a youngish fellow with a round, boyish face, arrives wearing a white hat, which he hangs on the hook behind us as he pulls up a stool. The older men start talking about the hat, which the young fellow explains is a family heirloom. "I like hats but I never wear them," says one of the older men. The waitress joins in: "I once wore hats all the time, but I kept losing them. If I go out drinking I forget them. I've got hats all over Tokyo." Another older man says, "If you're going out to get drunk you hardly need to wear a hat," and there's laughter. More laughter follows when the waitress says, "Kuni-san can't wear hats." Everyone knows what she will say next. "His head is too big."

"Pity there's nothing inside it," chips in a long-time regular. Unfortunately, Kuni is busy in his kitchen and I can't witness a rejoinder, but I know it would have been fast and funny.

Somebody asks to try on the hat and the young fellow removes it from the hook and passes it over. It is inspected closely and admired as a classic Panama model, then returned to its hook. One of the men remarks that such hats were popular in the Taisho Era. And I recall seeing such hats in an early Akira Kurosawa film, made in about the same year that Saiki began trading. "That's right," says the man. "*Nora Inu* (*Stray Dog*). I'd forgotten about that movie. Yes, those cops were very stylish." In a scene from the film, a group of detectives are practising at an outdoor firing range in midsummer, and through the black and white screen you can feel Tokyo's searing heat. But the cops are dressed for it, in loose-fitting white linen suits and trousers—and white hats.

I look again at the hat on the wall. It suits Saiki, its creamy whiteness offsetting the aged wooden interior burnished by years of cooking and tobacco, the loamy, olive-brown walls with their unique wear marks, like abstract paintings, where customers have leaned against them or repeatedly (how many thousand times?) hung and removed coats and scarves and bags, each time brushing a little of the wall surface away. The breeze flutters the blue noren and outside it grows dark, as we settle in to a couple of hours' gentle conversation.

Living history. The loamy walls at Saiki speak of the countless patrons who have taken a little of the izakaya home on their coats.

Fried Chicken Gizzards

Daikon radish is a palate cleanser, a stomach settler, and the perfect companion to the hearty crunch of these deep-fried gizzards.   *Recipe p. 56*

Fried Shrimp Quenelles

The gorgeous texture of these shrimp balls comes from the contrast between shrimp pieces, creamy shrimp and fish pastes, and the fluffiness of the mayonnaise, which becomes airy upon deep frying.   *Recipe p. 56*

Creamy Crab Croquettes

A heavenly comfort food with crisp breadcrumb coating and a filling reminiscent of a crab-infused béchamel sauce. If preferred, substitute tomato or Worcester sauce for tartar.   *Recipe p. 57*

Fried Chicken Gizzards

砂肝唐揚げ
Sunagimo Kara-age

P. 55

SERVES 4

1 lb. (450g) chicken gizzards (about ⅔ lb./300g after trimming)
2 tbsp. potato starch
4 tbsp. *ponzu* sauce *recipe p. 145

1½ cups grated *daikon* radish
2 tbsp. scallion, thinly sliced
Vegetable oil for deep frying

1. If the gizzards come with white membrane and skin, trim these away with a sharp knife. Rinse thoroughly in cold water and pat dry. In a large heavy saucepan, preheat the oil to 375°F (190°C). (The high temperature enables the gizzards to cook quickly—they toughen if overcooked.)

2. In a small bowl, toss the gizzards with potato starch. Fry for 4 minutes, turning from time to time to prevent sticking together. When the gizzards start floating to the surface, turn up the heat so that they appear drier and crispier. Continue frying until browned (the potato starch will stay white). Transfer to a paper-lined tray.

3. Spoon the grated daikon into small serving bowls and place the gizzards on top. Sprinkle with ponzu and sliced scallions. Mix well before eating.

Fried Shrimp Quenelles

海老しんじょ
Ebi Shinjo

P. 55

MAKES 4 quenelles

6 oz. (170g) shrimp, peeled, de-veined, rinsed and patted dry
6 oz. (170g) fillets of cod, pollock or haddock, boned
6 oz. (170g) onion, finely chopped

2 tsp. vegetable oil
3 oz. (85g) mayonnaise
½ tsp. salt
Mild chili pepper, such as Anaheim or *shishito*, skin pierced
Potato starch
Vegetable oil for deep frying

1. Chop ⅔ of the shrimp to a coarse paste and the remaining ⅓ roughly, into about ⅛ in. (3mm) pieces. Alternatively, pulse in a food processor or mash in a *suribachi* mortar (see glossary p. 155).

2. Using a food processor, pulse the fish fillet into a paste, adding a little water as needed to loosen the consistency. Alternatively, grind in a suribachi morter.

3. In a medium frying pan, heat the oil over medium high heat. Sauté the onion until golden brown, then cool at room temperature.

4. With a rubber spatula, mix the onion, all shrimp, fish paste, mayonnaise and salt. Refrigerate for ½ to 1 hour until the mixture is cold and firm enough to handle.

5. In a heavy saucepan, preheat the oil to 340°F (170°C). Fry the chili peppers (without batter) until soft. Transfer to a paper-lined dish.

6. Shape flat quenelles using two serving spoons or an ice cream scoop, dust with potato starch, then deep fry until they puff up and float to the surface of the oil. Increase the heat (to about 360°F/180°C) and continue frying until the quenelles appear crisp. Transfer to a paper-lined tray.

7. On a serving plate, arrange the quenelles with chili peppers on the side.

The tiny kitchen at Saiki accommodates two chefs during busy periods, serving two dozen customers. An impressive logistical feat, though not unusual in the world of izakaya.

Creamy Crab Croquettes

カニクリームコロッケ

Kani Kurimu Korokke

P. 55

MAKES 8 croquettes

4½ oz. (130g) fresh or
canned crabmeat,
cartilage removed
4 oz. (110g) onion, finely
chopped
1 tbsp. vegetable oil
1 large hard-boiled egg,
finely chopped

1 tsp. salt
¼ tsp. freshly ground black
pepper
Vegetable oil for deep frying
Tartar sauce
Lettuce, as garnish

White Sauce
- 1 oz. (30g) unsalted butter
- 1 oz. (30g) flour
- 1½ cup (360ml) or more whole milk, warmed

Breading
Flour, beaten eggs and *panko* breadcrumbs, in three separate dishes

1. In a large frying pan, heat the oil and sauté the onion
until lightly browned. Set aside.

2. For the white sauce, stir the butter and flour in a small
frying pan over low heat with a wooden spoon or whisk
to keep lumps from forming. Slowly pour in the milk,
stirring constantly to disperse the flour into the liquid.
Bring to a simmer and mix vigorously so that the mixture
doesn't brown and its floury taste is cooked off, about 5
minutes. It should have a firm mustard-like consistency.

2. In the large frying pan holding the sautéed onion, add
the crabmeat and cook off the moisture over medium heat,
for 3 minutes. Add the boiled egg and the white sauce,
then season with salt and pepper. Remove from heat.

3. When cool enough to handle, spread the mixture onto
a half-oven sheet and seal with plastic wrap. Chill in
refrigerator and allow to set for 1 hour.

4. Make flat-oval croquettes from the mixture, then
bread with the flour, egg and panko in turns. Try to bread
quickly so that your body temperature does not further
soften the patties.

5. Preheat the oil to 360°F (180°C). Slip the croquettes
into the oil and deep fry, without disturbing, until golden
brown. With a spider strainer, gently transfer to a paper-
lined dish. Arrange on a serving plate, garnish with lettuce and serve with tartar sauce.

RARE TASTES AND THE CURE

Most izakaya menus include the category *chinmi*:
literally, "rare taste." Meant to be enjoyed with
sake or *shochu*, these tiny, powerful dishes are
not for everyone. They encompass the heavily salted, fermented entrails of sea creatures including squid, bonito,
tuna, and sea slug. Even many Japanese dislike a fair
proportion of them. The most divisive dish is no doubt
hoya, or sea squirt, which at least a few of my acquain-
tances insist that no one in their right mind should eat.
Its texture is like that of many shellfish, though it packs
an acerbic, ammonia-like punch that has a somewhat
toxic, exciting sensation on the tongue. Indeed, few
other nibbles will have you reaching as quickly for a shot
of strong drink, and this is perhaps the point.

On a less odiferous level, although still challenging
for some, is the huge range of other fermented foods
offered by izakaya. If you like smoked seafood, you cannot go past the amino-acid-laden *umami* of semi-dried
fish (p.58). Soy sauce, *katsuobushi* bonito flakes, and
miso are all fermented foods, with the latter encourag-
ing healthy flora in your intestines. *Natto* fermented
soybeans may be hard to get used to, thanks to their
sliminess and strong smell, but there are very few foods
that are as good for you. It is worth making the effort.
Also healthful are long-cured pickles, or *tsukemono*,
which brim with lactobacillus and assist digestion, and
umeboshi, the deliciously sour, pickled plum that goes so
well with chicken, or simply on top of hot rice.

Skewered Pork Cutlets

Another satisfying, deep-fried snack that Saiki does so well. Pork cutlets are so popular in Japan that there are specialty stores which serve nothing else. Use tender pork. Delicious with shredded cabbage and hot mustard. *Recipe p. 60*

Overnight-dried Fish

There are countless ways of drying fish: in the sun, the shade, after soaking in sweet sake, or as shown here, overnight. The nutrients and flavor are powerfully intensified by drying, and the strong aroma released upon broiling sets fish lovers' mouths watering. *Recipe p. 60*

Sweet Miso-marinated Fish

This home-cooking standard has become a fad outside of Japan. Depending on preference, cook lightly or until the miso is slightly charred. Any kind of juicy, cod-like fish may be used.   *Recipe p. 61*

One of the most welcoming things about izakaya is the provision of hot or cold hand towels as soon as you sit down. Sadly this practice has grown less prevalent, but at Saiki the hospitality continues. Patrons even receive a fresh towel on exiting the bathroom.

Skewered Pork Cutlets

串カツ
Kushi-katsu

SERVES 4

P. 58

1 lb. (450g) pork loin, 1 in. (2.5cm) thick
1 medium yellow onion
Salt and black pepper
Cabbage, soaked in cold water to crisp, then julienned
Japanese hot mustard (wagarashi)
Worcester sauce
Oil for deep frying

Breading
Flour, beaten eggs, *panko* crumbs in three separate dishes

1. Cut the pork into 10 pieces. If you want nice fried skewers when cut in half, each cube should be approximately 1×1×2 in.(2.5×2.5×5cm).
2. Peel the onion and cut off both ends to 2 in. (5cm) thick. Cut the onion (horizontally) into even half rounds. Cut each half into 8 wedges.
3. Starting with an onion wedge, alternately thread the pork and onion pieces by their wider sides onto bamboo skewers. Each skewer should have three onion wedges and two pork pieces. Season generously with salt and pepper, then bread with flour, egg and panko.
4. Preheat the oil to 340°F (170°C). Deep fry the prepared skewers until slightly golden brown, for about 12 minutes. Increase the heat and continue frying to crisp them. Transfer to a paper-lined dish to drain excess oil. Remove the skewers with a twisting action, and cut the cutlets lengthwise into halves. Serve with the julienned cabbage, Japanese hot mustard and Worcester sauce.

Overnight-dried Fish

一夜干し
Ichiyaboshi

MAKES 1 whole dried fish

P. 58

1 whole fish about 8–12 in. (20–30 cm) long, such as *aji* horse mackerel, sardine, herring or small snapper
Sea salt
Grated *daikon* radish or lemon wedges
Soy sauce

3% Sea Salt Solution
⎡ 2 cups (480ml) water
⎣ 4 tsp. sea salt

1. To dry overnight: scale the fish if required. Remove gills and innards, then butterfly from the belly side or back side. Rinse away any blood under cold water and pat dry. In a flat container or a pot large enough to hold the whole fish, make the 3% sea-salt solution to cover the fish. Soak the fish for about 20 minutes, depending on its size, fattiness, and the room temperature (in summer with higher temperature and moisture, the fish should be brined in a refrigerator). Lightly pat dry and hang outside for approximately 4 to 6 hours, either in the sun or overnight. Your results will be better if a breeze is circulating.
2. To broil: place the fish on a mesh grill or cooking grate over a baking tray to collect drips. Broil flesh-side-up until the flesh becomes opaque and almost cooked, for 7–15 minutes depending on the fish. Flip the fish, and broil the other side for 3–5 minutes until the skin is browned in spots. Serve with a mound of grated daikon radish, soy sauce, or lemon wedge.

The Japanese body may have grown bigger over recent generations, but if old furniture and counter heights remain small, few patrons have trouble fitting in; indeed, the cramped conditions promote conviviality.

Sweet Miso-marinated Fish

魚の西京漬け
Sakana no Saikyo-zuke

SERVES 2

P. 59

2 fillets of *gindara* sable fish, cod or Spanish mackerel, preferably skin-on, ½ lb. (230g) each
Sea salt
2 cups (19 oz./550g) white miso
¾ cup (180ml) *mirin*
4 mild chili peppers, skin pierced and grilled

1. In a small saucepan, bring the mirin to a boil. Turn off heat, add the white miso and dissolve well. Cool to room temperature.
2. Lightly smear the fillets with salt. Put on a rack over a tray to collect drips, and place in refrigerator for 20 minutes. Rinse under cold water and pat dry with a paper towel.
3. In a flat-bottomed plastic storage container, slather the fish all over with the miso and cover with a lid. Leave in refrigerator to marinate for about a day.
4. To broil: Wipe off excess miso so that the fish is no more than lightly smeared. Broil both sides until the edges are browned and the flesh is cooked through. Serve with grilled chili peppers.

Saiki keeps things simple, stocking only a few varieties of *sake* and *shochu*. Lining the wall are earthenware shochu bottles. Regular customers may buy a bottle and store it here; some express their artistry with a felt-tip pen.

Sautéed Small Squid and Celery

Reminiscent of a Chinese stir-fry, the pieces of squid make this an ideal dish for sharing. Just dive in with your chopsticks. Use small, tender squid. The finishing flourish of garlic butter lends a special touch, or *kakushi-aji* (hidden taste).   *Recipe p. 64*

Deep-fried Eggplant in *Dashi* Marinade

This dish often appears on Saiki's menu as an *o-toshi* appetizer and harks back to Buddhist temple dishes that are deep fried without batter. Eggplant soaks up liquid readily, so use good fresh oil. Transfer to the *dashi* when hot, to absorb maximum flavor.   *Recipe p. 64*

Komatsuna Greens in *Dashi* and Soy Sauce

Make this easy dish with any in-season greens. Drizzle with *dashi* and soy sauce just before serving. The saltiness should not be overpowering.   *Recipe p. 64*

SLICED TOMATOES

The izakaya's charm steers conversation through delightful turns. Over the course of the evening, as you and your companions plot your meal, you will find dishes that revive memories or spur new thoughts.

I am sitting at Hiro (p. 106) with my friend Shigeru, who orders a dish of *hatsukoi tomato*. These tomatoes are different from the ultra-sweet, brix 9 variety that Hiro also offers, though they are served in the same way: nothing but sliced tomatoes, and a little mound of sea salt. Curious about the name, which means "first love," I ask Shigeru if he knows its origin. His facial expression suggests I have missed a vital part of my education. "Everyone knows that first love is sweet and sour," he says. "These tomatoes are like that." I had never thought of there being a consensus on the flavor of young romance, but the Japanese have reached one, and so Shigeru and I trade reminiscences of our distant-past relationships, and I come away with a new appreciation of my friend. All this from a sliced tomato.

Izakaya eating is almost as much about ideas and social intercourse as it is about cooking. Some dishes, such as the tomatoes, have no recipe. Here are some dead-easy snacks that will add color (and perhaps a talking point) to your pub-food spread.

- *Miso celery*: cut a stem of celery into sticks, peel off the ribs, and place in a plastic bag with a tablespoon of miso, and refrigerate for a few hours. Lightly rinse off the miso before serving.
- *Onion slices*: Finely slice an onion and soak in water. Drain and serve with a dressing of soy sauce and vinegar, topped with a generous amount of *katsuobushi* bonito flakes.
- Grilled *nagaimo* mountain yam: Cut an 8 in. (20cm) nagaimo tuber in half lengthwise. Grill the semi-circular lengths over charcoal or medium flame. Slice into large half-moons and serve with a mound of sea salt.
- *Asazuke* pickles: Rub vegetable pieces (cucumber, carrot, turnip, cabbage) generously with sea salt and ginger slivers, leave for 10 minutes, then lightly squeeze out excess water. Sprinkle with bonito flakes and soy sauce before eating.

Sautéed Small Squid and Celery

ひいかのセロリ炒め

Hika no Serori Itame

`SERVES` 4

P. 62

1 lb. (450g) small squid (calamari)
2 celery stalks, with leaves
2 tsp. vegetable oil
1 tbsp. garlic butter * recipe below
Salt and black pepper
2 lemon wedges

1. To clean the squid: with your hands, pull out the tentacles and separate flips (fins) from the bodies (mantle). Squeeze out the beak. Rinse the body, tentacles, and flips with cold water and pat dry.
2. Slice tentacles and flips into bite-sized pieces. Cut bodies crosswise into ¼ in. (6mm) thick rings. Slice the celery stalks and leaves into ¼ in. (6mm) thick pieces.
3. In a large frying pan, heat the oil over high heat for 1 minute. Add the squid, salt, and pepper, and sauté for 1 minute. Add the celery stalks, and when they are barely softened, add celery leaves. Adjust seasoning with salt and pepper.
4. Place on a serving dish with lemon wedge, and top with the garlic butter. Melt the butter with a kitchen torch.

Garlic Butter

1 garlic clove, finely chopped
¼ tsp. salt
4 tbsp. unsalted butter, softened to room temperature

1. On a clean cutting board, finely chop the garlic. Sprinkle the salt over the garlic and smear the garlic to a paste with the flat side of the knife against the cutting board. Transfer to a small bowl and mix well with the butter using a rubber spatula.
2. Transfer to a small container and refrigerate until firm.

Deep-fried Eggplant in *Dashi* Marinade

なす揚げびたし

Nasu Age-bitashi

`SERVES` 2

P. 62

2 Japanese eggplants
2–4 mild chili peppers such as Anaheim or *shishito*
Vegetable oil for deep frying

Marinade
⌈ ½ cup (120ml) *kaeshi* concentrate *recipe p. 117
│ 1 cup (240ml) water
⌊ 1 dried red chili pepper or 1 tsp. red chili pepper flakes

1. In a medium heavy saucepan, preheat the oil to 340°F (170°C). In a medium container, combine all marinade ingredients.
2. Cut off the stem end of each eggplant and slice lengthwise, about ¼ in. (6mm) thick. Pierce the skin of the chili peppers. Deep fry the eggplant and peppers until softened. Transfer onto a paper-lined dish to absorb excess oil. While still hot, soak in the marinade and leave for at least 30 minutes.
3. Arrange in small serving bowls.

Komatsuna Greens in *Dashi* and Soy Sauce

小松菜のおひたし

Komatsuna no O-hitashi

`SERVES` 2–4

P. 62

1 lb. (450g) *komatsuna* greens (substitutes include fresh spinach, mustard greens or Swiss chard), trimmed
Salt
3 tbsp. *dashi* stock *recipe p. 101
3 tbsp. soy sauce
Bonito flakes (*katsuo kezuri-bushi*), as garnish

Prepare ice water in a medium bowl. In a medium pot, bring salted water to a boil. Cook the greens briefly until crisp-tender, then drain and plunge into the ice water to stop cooking. Lightly squeeze out excess water and cut the greens into 2 in. (5cm) segments. Arrange in tight bunches in serving bowls. Combine dashi and soy sauce, pour over the greens and top with the bonito flakes.

JAPANESE AROMATICS

Japan is blessed with a variety of fresh herbs and seasonings that, until recently, were almost impossible to obtain abroad. Thanks to the popularity of Japanese cooking, the ingredients featured in this book should now be obtainable at many major markets, in your local Chinatown, or via the Internet. Here are some of the basics.

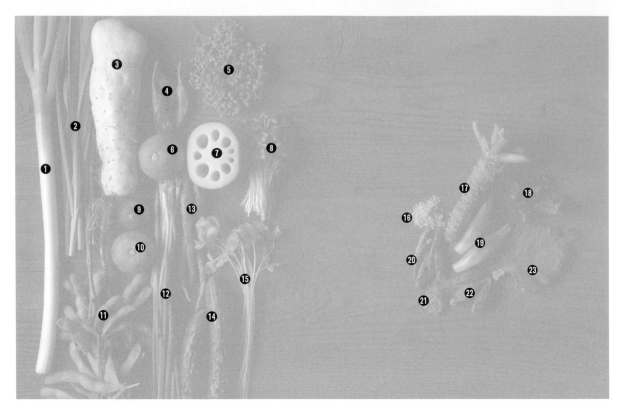

❶ *Naganegi* white scallion

Similar to Welsh onion or spring onion, this species, about the thickness of a medium cigar, has a mild onion flavor and is prized for its white stem (produced by growing in a raised "collar" of soil). It is often sliced into ultra-thin, silvery curls for garnishing soup, meat, and poultry dishes (see Sliced Duck Breast with *Ponzu* Sauce, p.143).

❶ *Nira* garlic chives

With its subtle, garlic-onion flavor, *nira* is stir fried or steamed with meat, added to soups or stews, or minced and used in dumplings. Also popular in Chinese and Korean cooking. Yellow nira, grown shielded from the sun, has a more delicate flavor.

❸ *Yamaimo* mountain yam

Also known as *tororo imo*, this is the oldest variety of potato in Japan, and is one of the Japanese diet's main *neba neba*, or mucilaginous, foods. It is most commonly grated and eaten raw, mixed with dashi stock, a dab of wasabi and a sprinkling of *nori* seaweed; or chopped into matchstick-like segments and treated like a salad vegetable. It is also used as a binding ingredient for minced fish or meat balls. Another variety, the *naga imo*, or long yam, is less slimy and therefore not used for binding, but its clean taste and crispness, when simply grilled over charcoal and eaten with a pinch of salt, is heavenly.

❹ *Shishito* pepper

This miniature, sweet, mildly hot pepper is typically deep fried whole as a garnish (p. 55), skewered, salted, and grilled (p. 59), or battered and served as tempura. Remember to pierce the skin before deep-frying, as they may burst in hot oil. Don't substitute similarly-shaped Serrano or Thai bird peppers, as they are extremely hot. Though a different size, Anaheim peppers are good substitute.

❺ *Sansho* peppercorns

A highly distinctive, tangy spice from the Japanese prickly ash tree, *sansho* is related to the Szechuan pepper. It has a clove-like numbing action on the tongue and is indispensable to offset the sweet richness of broiled eel. Also used to season grilled meats and fish. The leaves of the prickly ash, called *kinome*, are used as a garnish (P. 42, 98, 99).

❻ *Yuzu* citrus

The delicious aroma of this citrus fruit, a native of Asia, makes it a valuable ingredient either green in summer or ripe in winter, when it sweetens and turns yellow. Its juice evokes both grapefruit and mandarin. The zest is grated into dishes, mixed with ground meat (recipe p. 130), or combined with green chili to make the spicy condiment *yuzu-kosho* (recipe p. 145). The juice is used in dressings and sauces such as *ponzu* (recipe p. 145). During winter, yuzu are often floated in bathtubs. Be aware that yuzu's distinctive, powerful flavor can tempt one into overusing it—I confess that when I first discovered yuzu-kosho I smeared it on almost everything, with some ignoble results—so go sparingly.

❼ *Renkon* lotus root

Every part of the lotus can be eaten, and the root is tastiest in winter. It has a nutty, starchy taste and crunchy, juicy texture. The holes in the root are seen by the Japanese as lucky, since one can peer through them and "see the future." The root can be sliced and its holes stuffed with ground meat before deep frying as in the dish *renkon no hasami age*, or sliced paper-thin and mixed with vegetables in a salad (p. 39).

❽ *Kaiware*, *daikon* radish sprouts

Kaiware means literally, "split shells," and this herb is so named because of its split seed pods upon sprouting. Kaiware are peppery and fresh tasting, slightly bitter like *daikon*, and rich in minerals and phytochemicals. Wash well before using.

9 *Sudachi* citrus

This tight-fleshed small citrus, typically weighing around 1 oz. (30g.), has a flavor somewhere between lemon and lime. Sudachi is often drizzled over fish or *matsutake* mushrooms, and is served in wedges to squeeze into dipping sauces of *somen* or *udon* noodles.

10 *Kabosu* citrus

Bigger than the *sudachi* but used in the same way, the kabosu is married in the Japanese diner's mind to charcoal-grilled *sanma*, or Pacific saury, for the fish and fruit come into season together, in September/October.

11 *Edamame* fresh green soybeans

It has been a decades-long mystery to me, since I first enjoyed these summer beans with a cold beer, why their popularity as a drinking snack was not massive and world-wide. Not only delicious and refreshing, but a healthy alternative to nibbles like fried chips, soybeans are satisfying to eat when popped from their pods straight into your mouth. They are available frozen, though fresh is far superior. Boil in lightly salted water for 3-4 minutes., then drain and sprinkle with mineral-rich sea salt. Some cooks choose to cut them from their branches before preparing—with scissors, cut each pod about ⅛ in. (3mm) below its top—while others like to retain the decorative feel of the stalks, trimming them just enough to fit the serving bowl, and so that guests can pull off their own pods, or pick up a branch bearing several pods.

12 *Aonegi* green scallion

A ubiquitous garnish, this scallion comes in numerous regional varieties and thicknesses. On average, the stems are about as thick as a pencil, but some varieties will be as thin as chives. These look beautiful sliced very finely and set floating in clear soup. Aonegi tend to be sweeter and juicier than the naganegi white scallion, with a stronger onion aroma.

13 *Amanaga* pepper

Literally, "sweet and long," the amanaga is milder than the shishito pepper. It is used as a garnish and is popular in *kaiseki* cuisine, and with its contrasting taste and texture, makes an attractive component of such dishes as Yamariki's Grilled Green Salad (p. 100). The Anaheim pepper is a good substitute.

14 *Kyuri* Japanese cucumber

About 7 in. (18cm) long and 1 in. (2.5cm) thick, the Japanese cucumber is succulent and need not (in fact, *should not*) be peeled or seeded. It is eaten countless ways, sometimes simply chilled and skewered whole, for sale at summer festivals (think a healthy Dagwood dog), or sliced into a fan shape to soak up a vinegar dressing (p. 16). Substitute English or Mediterranean cucumbers.

15 *Mitsuba* leaves

Often compared to watercress, parsley or coriander, mitsuba is, as with so many Japanese seasonings, like nothing else. Pungent, refreshing, delicate and a little bitter, it is a unique garnish. It is often hydroponically grown and comes in three forms: *ito-mitsuba* for clear soups; *ne-mitsuba*—the strongest flavored—is blanched and prepared as a chilled appetizer; and *kiri-mitsuba*, the most subtle and tender variety, for garnishing.

16 *Wagarashi* Japanese hot mustard

Buy Japanese powdered mustard in small tins, and mix equal amounts of powder and water. Alternatively, buy ready-made in a tube. A dab of Japanese mustard is served with grilled meats (the izakaya Yamariki uses Colman's), mixed into dressings, and whipped with soy sauce and scallions together with *natto* fermented soybeans.

17 *Wasabi* root

It should be fairly well known by now that the vast majority of what is passed off as *wasabi*, in restaurants and supermarkets in Japan and abroad, is not wasabi at all but a concoction of Western horseradish, mustard powder and green/yellow dye. The reason for this is that wasabi is very difficult to grow, requiring large amounts of pristine, flowing water and a just-right climate. If you are lucky enough to find fresh wasabi root (strictly speaking not a root but a rhizome), grate from the stem side and prepare only as much as you need, directly before use. Wasabi's volatile oils quickly dissipate as they oxidize. Serious chefs use a sharkskin grater, believing the softer nature of this material brings out more flavor by crushing the wasabi fibers, rather than cutting them, as the teeth of a metal grater will do. And if you can't find fresh wasabi, don't fret—at least the Western horseradish is a relative (but then again, so is the cabbage!).

18 *Kikurage* wood ear mushrooms

So named for its resemblance to ears, *kikurage* tree fungus is readily available dried (most comes from China) and after soaking is shredded or sliced for use in stir-fried dishes and soups. It has a delightful crunchy, gelatinous texture, which it retains throughout cooking.

19 *Myoga* "Japanese ginger"

Native to Japan and related to ginger, *myoga* buds are rather like a flower whose magenta-green "petals" are eaten raw or grilled, sliced or whole—as at the Morimoto *yakitori* pub (p. 121), where it is smeared with *miso* before broiling. Myoga has a tart, gingery flavor and is also used finely shredded as a garnish.

20 *Taka no tsume* dried chili

Japanese cuisine is rarely spicy hot, but this universal ingredient is essential to making the grated *daikon* radish condiment *momiji oroshi* (p. 20), various pickle dishes, and in stir fries.

21 *Shichimi* spice powder

Another ubiquitous, spicy condiment. Pour a small mound on your *yakitori* plate and dip the grilled morsels as you eat, or sprinkle lightly on almost any cooked dish or noodle dipping sauce. *Shichimi* is usually a blend of the following seven (the name means "seven flavors") ingredients: red chili powder, dried orange peel, black sesame seeds, hemp seeds, ginger powder, powdered mustard seeds, and powdered *sansho*.

22 *Kuchinashi no mi* gardenia fruit

Cracked slightly open, gardenia fruit are used to naturally color sweet potatoes, *takuan* radish pickles, noodles and other foods.

23 *Shiso* perilla leaves

Often described as "Japanese basil," this sour, minty, refreshing herb goes well with salt and soy sauce and, served whole, is a digestive aid when eaten with *sashimi* (along with *daikon* radish). Its tiny bell-like flower buds are also used to garnish sashimi—simply stroke them off the branch into your soy sauce dish. The leaf is julienned for use in salads or dressings. From June to July shiso leaves turn red, and are used for coloring and flavoring *umeboshi* pickled plums. The leaf is sometimes battered and deep fried as tempura, and is also essential to the *yakitori* favorite *Ume shiso* (p. 130).

シンスケ

TIME AND
AGAIN

シンスケ Shinsuke

A classic summer dish of old Tokyo is *dojo*, or loaches. In one popular recipe, the tiny freshwater fish are deep fried alive, and if this seems brutal the Japanese at least acknowledge it, by means of an atoning ritual. Of course not all chefs observe this, but one man who certainly does is Naoharu Yabe, the fourth generation master of Shinsuke, one of Tokyo's finest working-class neighborhood izakaya. Everything about Shinsuke expresses its status as the ultimate Tokyo-style pub, from its simple yet elegant artisan-crafted interior, to its exclusively produced *sake*, to its outstanding menu—created by a team of thirteen, including Yabe's mother and father.

When Shinsuke purchases its first loaches of the summer, Yabe takes a fifth of them and releases them in a local pond. "It's our way of praying for their souls," he says. "And to apologize for putting them into the hell of hot oil." In a further gesture, the luckless remaining fish are anaesthetized in a bath of sake before cooking, and it is not just any rice brew, but top quality *daiginjo* sake. I doubt whether the loaches care about which grade of alcohol makes them blotto, but for the chef wishing to atone, the distinction is important.

Tradition counts for much at Shinsuke, not as a crusty specter of the past, but as a continuous life force. This is the essence of the downtown Tokyo sensibility. Life flows

71

ter and the pub's history. The exterior, with its vertical row of wooden slats spanning the windows across the entire length of the building, provides privacy and also, through the light that leaks out, a sense of warm invitation. It is classically old Japan, as is the *sakabayashi* hanging ball of trimmed cedar branches in the doorway, a mark of respect to the sake gods. The *noren* shop curtain is not the typical indigo-dyed split cloth but a row of plaited reeds, considered airier and less highbrow, according to Toshio Yabe.

Inside, Naoharu is the boss, engaging customers, talking readily about his menu and bustling to serve. His father, dressed in a meticulously tailored, striped *happi* coat of fine fabric that manages to look extremely casual, and on his head a twisted cloth *hachimaki*, is in charge of warming the sake. He doesn't seem to do a lot more, hanging back and occasionally prodding his son when, for example, he considers customers have been waiting too long for their appetizers, but the way he oversees everything puts you at ease.

The secret of Shinsuke's appeal may be that the staff honor you to exactly the same degree that they honor their work and their establishment. As Yabe says, "We are just the backstage workers. The izakaya is the stage and the customers have the main role." In this finely crafted room, with the intimacy of a personal kind of shrine, you may feel this is one of Tokyo's greatest pleasures.

Spinach with Black Sesame Sauce

The inspiration for this rich play of black on green may come from master Naoharu Yabe's study of pottery and tea ceremony. That's what Yabe himself thinks. The sauce is not a uniformly smooth paste, as the roughness of crushed sesame lends a home-style touch. *Recipe p. 76*

"Lightning Bolt" *Shirouri* Summer Squash Pickles

Early summer, the season for *shirouri* squash, is also the season for thunderstorms in Tokyo, hence the name of this traditional Edo pickle. The curls look rather like lightning bolts, and even crackle when you bite them. If you cannot find *shirouri*, a similar-textured pickle can be made with chayote, or choko, though the shape will be different. *Recipe p. 76*

Spinach with Black Sesame Sauce

ほうれん草の胡麻和え

Horenso no Goma-ae

P. 74

`SERVES` 4

1½ pounds (680g) bunch spinach, thoroughly washed and trimmed
Toasted white sesame seeds, as garnish

Sesame sauce
1 tbsp. black tahini paste
1 tbsp. black sesame seed
2 tbsp. granulated sugar
1½ tbsp. soy sauce
2 tsp. *dashi* stock *recipe p. 101
1 tbsp. *mirin*

1. For the sesame sauce: lightly toast the sesame seeds in a small frying pan until fragrant and grind them in a *suribachi* (glossary p. 155) or food processor. Add the sugar and continue grinding. Combine with the tahini, soy sauce, dashi stock and mirin (use dashi to adjust the consistency to that of a loose peanut butter).
2. In a large pot, bring salted water to a boil. Cook spinach until tender but crisp, about 1 minute. Shock with ice water, drain, then with stems bunched together gently wring out excess water. Cut into 1½ in. (4cm) lengths. For a neater shape, as shown, use a bamboo sushi rolling mat, lay the squeezed spinach in it, roll lightly, and cut into 1½ in. (4cm) lengths.
3. Arrange in a serving bowl, spoon the sesame sauce over, and sprinkle with toasted white sesame seeds.

"Lightning Bolt" *Shirouri* Summer Squash Pickles

白瓜かみなり干し

Shirouri Kaminari Boshi

P. 75

`MAKES` ¾ cup

1 *shirouri* summer squash
White sesame seeds, toasted, optional

Brine
1 heaping teaspoon sea salt
1 cup (240ml) water

1. On a cutting board, sprinkle the shirouri squash with salt and roll it against the board to remove its fuzz. Rinse with cold water. Cut off both ends, cut in half crosswise and core the halves. Taking one half at a time and using a sharp paring knife with its tip at a 45° angle, carve the halves into a continuous ¼ in. (6mm) thick ribbon by turning the shirouri towards the blade (handle the ribbon gently to avoid splitting).
2. In a medium bowl, make the brine and soak the ribbons until lightly salted, about 1–2 hours.
3. Hang the ribbons to dry in a place where a breeze is circulating, until the skin is a little wrinkled, about 3 hours.
4. Cut into 2 in. (5cm) lengths and arrange on serving dishes. Sprinkle with toasted white sesame seeds.

For generations, Shinsuke has staked its name on serving an honest cup (a measure of 1-*go*, or 180ml) of *sake*. The izakaya still uses its ancient *masu* or wooden sake cup (on the left) to fill its flasks. A less generous measure, used by some other pubs, is shown beside it.

Tuna with *"Nuta"* Miso-Mustard Dressing

You can also use *wakame* seaweed and/or shellfish in this traditional dish. Nuta dressing is typically sweet and rich; the addition of hot mustard lightens the flavor. Use the green uppers of large scallions if available.   *Recipe p. 80*

Fried Tofu Stuffed with Raclette Cheese

A common filling for toasted, deep-fried tofu pockets is *natto* fermented soybeans. As far as I know, Shinsuke is the only place you will find them stuffed with Swiss Raclette cheese. This cross-cultural dish works beautifully.   *Recipe p. 80*

Mashed Potato Salad with Mayonnaise

This izakaya and home-cooking favorite gets the
luxury treatment in Shinsuke's recipe. You can sim-
plify, but letting the hot potatoes absorb the sake
and pickling liquid gives them a depth of flavor
before the addition of mayonnaise. Pickled ginger
provides a pleasant bite. *Recipe p. 81*

At Shinsuke's entrance is a big brown ball, *sakabayashi*. It is usually seen outside *sake* stores
and breweries, and is made of cedar leaves and
branches. Green when first hung, it is both an
offering to the sake gods and a sign that a new
sake season has begun. The *noren* shop curtain
is made of woven rushes. Yabe's father says it is
more casual than the cloth noren—easy to fling
aside in the carefree Edo style.

Tuna with *"Nuta"* Miso-Mustard Dressing

まぐろぬた

Maguro Nuta

`SERVES` 4   P. 74

5 oz. (140g) sashimi grade tuna in blocks or steaks
1 bunch (4 oz./115g) scallions or *wakegi* green onions
½ *udo* stalk or 1–2 stalks blanched white asparagus

Nuta Miso-mustard Dressing

⌈ 3 tbsp. white miso   1 tbsp. rice vinegar
⌊ 2⅔ tbsp. mirin   1 tsp. mustard powder

1. For the miso-mustard dressing: In a small cup or ramekin, blend the mustard powder to a paste with an equal amount of lukewarm water and set aside. Alternatively, use prepared Japanese mustard paste from a tube. Mix in the white miso, mirin, and rice vinegar.
2. Cut away the white stems of the scallion and any wilted green part. Have ready ice water in a medium bowl. In a medium saucepan, bring salted water to a boil. Briefly cook the scallion until tender, about 30 seconds. Shock in iced water and drain. On a cutting board, gently stroke or roll out the scallions with a rolling pin or the spine of a knife, to squeeze out as much water as possible. Cut into 1½ in. (4cm) lengths.
3. Thinly slice the udo stalk into ½×1½ in. (1.25×4cm) rectangles. Soak in vinegared water to prevent discoloring. Drain.
4. Cut the tuna into ¾ in. (about 2cm) cubes. Gently mix together the nuta dressing, tuna, scallions and udo stalk. Arrange in serving bowl.

Fried Tofu Stuffed with Raclette Cheese

きつねラクレット

Kitsune Rakuretto

`SERVES` 4   P. 79

8 deep-fried tofu pouches (*abura-age*)
4 slices Raclette cheese, same size as the tofu squares and about ¼ in. (6mm) thick
2 scallions
4 spiced prunes *recipe below

1. Deep-fried tofu squares range in size. If using about 3 in. (7.5cm) squares, just cut one side of the tofu and make a pouch. If using bigger rectangular fried tofu pouches, cut the center crosswise into halves.
2. Finely chop the white part of the scallions. Stuff into the tofu pouches along with the cheese. Thinly slice the green part of the scallions and set aside.
3. Broil the stuffed tofu pouches until the top is golden brown and the cheese is melted. Place on a serving plate and sprinkle with the chopped green scallion. Arrange four prunes on the side.

Spiced Prunes

`MAKES` 20 prunes

20 dried prunes, pitted
¾ cup (180ml) dry red wine
3 tbsp. sugar
2 in. (5cm) cinnamon stick

In a small saucepan, combine the red wine, sugar and cinnamon stick. Bring to a simmer, dissolve the sugar and flambé (or just simmer longer to evaporate alcohol). Add the prunes and simmer for 20 minutes.

Mashed Potato Salad with Mayonnaise

ポテトサラダ
Poteto Sarada

P. 79

SERVES 4

1 carrot
1 tbsp. unsalted butter
1 tbsp. granulated sugar
3 medium russet potatoes
3 tbsp. ginger pickles with pickling liquid *recipe below
1 tbsp. *sake*, preferably *daiginjo* style
¾ cup (170g) cucumber pickles *recipe below
8 thick slices ham, cut into bite-size pieces
¾ cup mayonnaise *recipe below
Freshly ground black pepper

1. Peel the carrots and cut into bite-size pieces. In a medium saucepan, add the carrots and barely cover with water. Bring to a simmer and cook for 10 minutes. Add the butter and sugar, and cook another 10 minutes until tender. Set aside.
2. In a large pot with boiling salted water, cook the potatoes until tender, then peel. While still hot, place in a large bowl and mash the potatoes to your liking. Add the ginger pickles with pickling liquid (see below) and sake and cool to room temperature.
3. When the mashed potato is cooled, combine with the carrots, pickled cucumbers and chopped ham. Season to taste with the mayonnaise. Top with freshly ground black pepper when serving.

Ginger Pickles

1 tbsp. small-diced ginger
3 tbsp. rice vinegar
2 tbsp. granulated sugar
1 tbsp. *dashi* stock *recipe p. 101
A pinch of sea salt

In a small non-reactive saucepan, combine the rice vinegar, granulated sugar, dashi stock and salt and bring to a boil. Cool to room temperature. Meanwhile, blanch the diced ginger, drain, and then pickle in the liquid for at least a day. For the mashed potato salad, both ginger and pickling liquid are used.

Cucumber Pickles

5 Japanese cucumbers
Sea salt
Piece of dried *kombu* kelp, 2 in. (5cm) square

Cut the cucumber in half lengthwise and cut into oblique slices. Put the kombu in a glass baking dish, and spread the cucumber over in single layer. Sprinkle with salt, lay a sheet of plastic wrap on top and weight with a flat-bottomed dish or similar. Refrigerate for a day, mixing occasionally. Before use, lightly drain any excess moisture.

Mayonnaise

1 large egg yolk
1½ tbsp. mustard powder
1¼ cup (300ml) vegetable oil
½ cup (120ml) rice vinegar or apple vinegar
1 tsp. salt

Dissolve the mustard with an equal amount of water. Combine the mustard paste, egg yolk and salt in a medium glass bowl. Blend with a whisk. Add oil a drop at a time, whisking constantly. If the mixture breaks up, start over with new ingredients. As the mixture thickens into mayonnaise, add vinegar and continue whisking, adding remaining oil generously. Adjust seasoning to taste. Store in refrigerator for up to 4 days.

Simmered Flounder, Edo Style

Flounder is a lean fish that should be seasoned with care and cooked quickly. Keep the stock simmering, as letting the temperature drop will stop the coagulation of protein on the fish's surface, creating a fishy odor.   *Recipe p. 84*

Deep-fried Sardine Rocks

Yabe's mother created these "rocks" based on an old Edo recipe. Use the freshest and fattest sardines you can find. The fish are not processed but finely chopped, giving the rocks an airy texture.   *Recipe p. 85*

Mizuna Salad with *Jako* Dried Baby Sardines

This unusual and invigorating salad delivers a delightful range of tastes and textures. The *kakushi-aji*, or "hidden taste," is *yuzu-kosho* citrus-pepper paste in the dressing. If you cannot find jako sardines, substitute a small amount of fried bacon or fried onions. *Recipe p. 85*

Tatsuta Fried Chicken

This soy-marinated chicken dish is another national favorite. Its name comes from the red-brown color of autumn leaves floating on the Tatsuta River, in the ancient capital of Nara.   *Recipe p. 84*

Simmered Flounder, Edo Style

江戸前かれい煮

Edo-mae Karei-ni

MAKES 1 medium flounder P. 82

1 whole flounder (about 7 oz./200g, 10in./25cm long), scaled and gutted from behind the gills
3 tbsp. *sake*
1 tsp. salt
Grated ginger, as garnish
Kinome sprigs, optional

Simmering stock

2 cups (480ml) *dashi* stock *recipe p. 101	2 tsp. sugar
⅓ cup (80ml) *mirin*	2–3 thin slices of ginger
⅓ cup (80ml) soy sauce	

1. Wash the flounder under running cold water and pat dry. To remove any fish odor, dissolve the salt into the sake and sprinkle on the flounder. Lay the fish on a fine-mesh rack and let drip for 20 minutes. It is unnecessary to wash or dry the flounder again. (This is a classic technique for removing fish odor. The mixture is called *sakashio*.)
2. Lay the fish on a cutting board, dark skin side up. With a sharp knife, make a long slash along the backbone so that the flounder cooks evenly. Mix the simmering stock ingredients in a large shallow pan or adequate sized casserole. Place the flounder into the pan and simmer it with a drop-lid (see glossary p. 153) until the flounder is cooked through, about 3–5 minutes. Place the flounder on a serving plate and spoon the simmering liquid over. Top with a dab of grated ginger and kinome sprigs.

Tatsuta Fried Chicken

若鶏の竜田揚げ

Wakadori no Tatsuta-age

SERVES 4 P. 82

1¼ lb. (570g) boneless chicken thigh, skin-on
1½ tsp. salt
3 tbsp. *sake*
½ zucchini, as garnish
Lemon wedges, as garnish
Vegetable oil for deep frying

Breading

Soy sauce and potato starch

1. Preheat the oil to 340°F (170°C). Cut chicken thigh into bite-size chunks. (Holding the knife at a 30-degree angle, cut the chicken across the grain. This gives a softer texture when fried.)
2. Place the chicken thigh and salt in a medium bowl and mix by rubbing well by hand. Add sake and repeat rubbing.
3. Prepare the soy sauce and potato starch in a small bowl. Dress the chicken pieces with soy sauce, dust with the starch, and deep fry until crispy, about 3–5 minutes. Transfer onto a paper-lined dish to drain excess oil.
4. Core the zucchini and cut into ⅓ in. (1cm) thick rounds. Deep fry (without batter) until tender but crispy, and transfer onto a paper-lined dish to drain excess oil.
5. Arrange the chicken on a serving plate with the fried zucchini and lemon wedges.

You can't improve on perfection. A classic, thick-glass soy sauce bottle sums up the Shinsuke aesthetic.

Deep-fried Sardine Rocks

いわしの岩石揚げ

Iwashi no Ganseki-age

P. 82

MAKES 8 cakes

12 large whole fresh sardines, about 1⅔ 1b. (725g) total
¼ small yellow onion, minced

A ⎡ 3 scallions, minced
⎜ 6 *shiso* leaves, minced
⎜ ¼ tsp. minced ginger
⎜ 1 large egg yolk, beaten
⎜ 2 tbsp. potato starch
⎜ 1 tbsp. yellow miso
⎣ ⅛ tsp. hot mustard

Mild chili peppers, such as Anaheim or *shishito*, skin pierced
2 tbsp. grated ginger

1. Cut off the heads of the sardines, remove entrails and wash thoroughly. Fillet and remove skin. With a sharp knife (a *deba* knife is best), mince the fillets. Alternatively, pulse into small chunks in a food processor. Transfer to a sieve and lightly drain excess water.
2. Preheat the oil to 320°F (160°C). In a large bowl, combine the chopped sardines, onion, and **A**. Mix well by hand. Shape into 8 small cones and deep fry until the cones rise to the surface of the oil and are well browned, about 7–10 minutes. Transfer to a paper-lined dish to drain excess oil.
3. Deep fry the mild chili peppers and transfer to a paper-lined dish.
4. Arrange the fried sardine cones on a serving plate. Serve with the chili peppers and grated ginger on the side.

Mizuna Salad with *Jako* Dried Baby Sardines

水菜とじゃこのサラダ

Mizuna to Jako no Salada

P. 82

SERVES 4

1 large bunch *mizuna* greens, yield
  to 4 cups
3 tbsp. *Jako* dried baby sardines
1 *yurine* lily bulb, about 5 oz. (140g)
Vegetable oil for frying

Dressing
⎡ 4 tbsp. grapeseed oil
⎜ 3–4 tbsp. fresh *yuzu* citrus juice or lemon juice
⎜ 1½ tbsp. finely grated onion
⎜ 1 tsp. *yuzu-kosho* citrus pepper paste *recipe p. 145
⎜ Several drops of soy sauce
⎣ Salt

1. To clean lily bulb: Break up the bulb into individual "petals" by hand, taking care not to split them. Trim away any grit or bruising. Rinse under cold running water.
2. Plunge mizuna greens in ice water to crisp, about 30 minutes.
3. Meanwhile, in a medium frying pan, heat ½ in. (1.25cm) of the oil to 320°F (160°C). Fry the *jako* baby sardines until lightly browned. Using a fine mesh skimmer, remove the jako from the oil and transfer to a paper-lined dish to drain excess oil.
4. For the dressing: Combine the citrus juice, the grated onion, yuzu-kosho and soy sauce in a small bowl. Add grapeseed oil, a little by little, to emulsify. Adjust with salt to taste.
5. Drain mizuna greens, blot dry with a clean paper towel and cut into 2½ in. (6.5cm) lengths.
6. Arrange the mizuna greens and lily bulb petals on a serving plate, spooning the dressing over. Top with the fried jako.

The *yurine* lily bulb has a warm and smooth potato-like texture and flavor. It can be steamed or eaten raw, and is becoming increasingly popular outside of Asia.

GUTS

カシラ
ビール
焼酎
酒
軟骨
タン
目
ハ
ツ
ガ
レ
バ

山利喜 Yamariki

Y ou can't miss Yamariki, the lively iza-kaya at the main intersection of blue-collar Morishita, eastern Tokyo, where a queue of eager diners waits for entry amid aromatic smoke from the charcoal grill inside. Above the door hangs a shop curtain showing a cartoon depiction of a pig, indicating the heart, liver, intestines and other organs. The pig prances happily on its hind legs while balancing a tray of drinks on one front hoof and gripping a skewer of grilled offal in the other. Yamariki was one of Tokyo's first izakaya, in the aftermath of World War II, to promote the eating of such animal parts. The second-generation master, Yoichi Yamada, tells me he thought up the cartoon pig from his desire to educate customers about the location of each pig part. "I remember grilled pork being sold at food stands before the war," he says. "But I wanted to sell organ meats, and people who went to fancy places had no idea where they came from. So I got the idea from my son's school textbook, to make a picture."

It's not only pork. The biggest seller at Yamariki is the pub's famous *motsu nikomi* stew of beef guts. In giant cauldrons, the sliced small intestines and fourth stomach of the cow are simmered together with boiled eggs in a dark, rich soup that has been kept on the boil, more or less, for some fifty years. The seasoning is red miso paste, red wine,

Asparagus and Pork Tempura Rolls

You may want to use toothpicks to hold these rolls together while cooking. Eat by dipping into the runny poached egg . . . gorgeous.

Recipe p. 92

Soy-flavored Spare Ribs

Spare ribs are not widely eaten in Japan, but when available, are generally large and meaty. This is a classic marinade incorporating *sake*, *mirin*, and soy sauce. The recipe overleaf is for the smaller rib racks.   *Recipe p. 92*

If you ever want to quaff a robust French wine while eating char-grilled pork organs, or knock back a Guiness with, say, a salt-broiled squid, this is the place to come. Yamariki boasts two sommeliers and a cellar enhanced by master Yamada's "food study" trips abroad.

Summer Scallop Salad with Spicy Tomato Sauce

Just looking at this dish makes me feel happy. A touch of Tabasco in the dressing lends some kick. As an alternative to scallops, use a light white fish, or quickly boiled shrimp, or crab.   *Recipe p. 93*

Asparagus and Pork Tempura Rolls

アスパラの肉巻き衣揚げ

Aspara no Nikumaki-age

8 large asparagus spears
About 8 or more thin
    slices of fresh pork belly
    (method in step 3)
1 lb. (450g) spinach
¼ tsp. vegetable oil
2–4 cherry tomatoes,
    halved, for garnish

1½ tbsp grated. Parmigiano-
    Reggiano cheese
4 poached eggs *recipe
    below
Vegetable oil for deep frying
Sea salt
Freshly ground black pepper

Batter
⌈ 1 cup (4 oz./125g) cake flour
| 1 cup (240ml) ice cold water
⌊ 2 tbsp. cornstarch

1. Cook the spinach in salted boiling water until tender-crisp, shock in ice water and squeeze out excess water. Cut into 2 in. (5cm) lengths and set aside.
2. Trim the tough ends of the asparagus and peel the stalk bottoms if necessary.
3. For the pork slices, placing the pork block in the freezer for 20 minutes before slicing will make cutting easier. Use a sharp knife. You may need a couple of slices to wrap each asparagus spear. As shown here, slices approximately 8×2×⅛ in. (200×50×3mm) were used.
4. Heat the vegetable oil to 340°F (170°C). Place an asparagus spear at the edge of a pork slice and tightly roll it around the asparagus. Continue until the asparagus is covered except for the tip. You may wish to fix the pork in place with a toothpick. Put asparagus aside, seal side down, and repeat with the remaining spears. Barely mix all the ingredients of the batter in a small bowl. The batter should be under-mixed and look lumpy. Dip the rolls in the batter and deep fry until golden and crispy, then transfer to a paper-lined dish to drain excess oil. Cut in halves or thirds.
6. Lay the boiled spinach on a serving plate. Arrange the fried rolls and place the cherry tomatoes, poached eggs, and a mixture of salt and pepper on the side. Sprinkle with the grated cheese.

Poached Eggs

¼ cup distilled white vinegar
½ teaspoon salt
4 large eggs

In a medium pot, pour in 6 in. (15cm) of water and bring to a bare simmer, with occasional tiny bubble forming. Add the vinegar (this helps the outer layer of the egg to congeal faster and so the eggholds shape). Crack an egg into a cup and carefully slide it into the water. When the water returns to a simmer, quickly repeat with all the eggs, spacing them apart. Gently simmer until whites are firm but yolks are still runny, about 3–4 minutes. Using a slotted spoon, transfer the eggs to paper towels to drain.

Soy-flavored Spare Ribs

和風スペアリブ

Wafu Supearibu

1½ lbs. (680g) pork rib racks
1 small orange, sliced, for garnish
Sprigs of curly parsley, for garnish

Marinade
⌈ 3 tbsp. soy sauce   1 garlic clove, sliced
| 2 tbsp. *sake*   ¼ small yellow onion,
| 2 tbsp. *mirin*   sliced
⌊ 1 tbsp. toasted sesame oil

1. Cut the rib racks between the bones into individual ribs. In a large bowl, combine all marinade ingredients. Add the ribs, toss to coat, and cover with plastic wrap. Refrigerate overnight or at least 6 hours.
2. Preheat the oven to 350°F (175°C). Place the ribs in a single layer on an aluminum foil-lined baking sheet. Brush with some of the remaining marinade and bake for 15 minutes. Flip once and bake another 15 minutes until the ribs are well browned and crispy on the upper edges.
3. While hot, arrange the ribs on a serving plate with the orange slices and sprigs of curly parsley.

Summer Scallop Salad with Spicy Tomato Sauce

帆立といんげんのピリ辛サラダ

Hotate to Ingen no Pirikara Sarada

SERVES 4

P. 91

10 large fresh sea scallops, sashimi grade
Iceberg lettuce, cut into bite-size pieces
Leaf lettuce, cut into bite-size pieces
Radicchio, cut into bite-size pieces
Celery, thinly sliced
Onion, thinly sliced
Green beans, trimmed, cooked in salted water and cut into 1
   in. (2.5cm) pieces

Marinade
¼ cup (60ml) extra virgin olive oil
Fresh lemon juice from 3 lemons
½ tsp. salt

Spicy Tomato Sauce
2 vine-ripened tomatoes, *concasse* *see Step 2
1⅓ tbsp. red wine vinegar
Hot pepper sauce, such as Tabasco, to taste
Salt and pepper
¼ cup (60ml) extra virgin olive oil
1 red bell pepper, chopped
1 yellow bell pepper, chopped
½ small celery stalk, chopped
1 Japanese cucumber or ⅓ English cucumber, unpeeled
   and chopped

1. Slice the scallops horizontally into ¼ in. (6mm) thick slices. In a container, make the marinade and dress the scallop slices. Cover with plastic wrap and marinate for 30 minutes in refrigerator.
2. For tomato concasse: bring water to rapid boil in a small saucepan. Have ready ice water in a small bowl. With a sharp paring knife, score a small crisscross on the bottom of each tomato, plunge in boiling water for 5 seconds and shock in ice water. Peel the skin away with a paring knife. Cut into wedges, remove seeds, and cut into small dice. Reserve any juices and add to the sauce.
3. In a cup, whisk the red wine vinegar, hot pepper sauce, and salt and pepper to taste. Gradually whisk in the olive oil so that it emulsifies. In a medium bowl, combine the tomato concasse, bell peppers, celery and cucumber. Toss with the red wine vinaigrette.
4. In a large bowl, combine the lettuces, radicchio, celery, onions and green beans. Arrange on a serving plate, top with the sliced scallops, and spoon the spicy tomato sauce over.

ETIQUETTE

Izakaya generally welcome all comers, but there are a few unwritten rules. I stress, however, that the etiquette is often situational.

The "clean" way to transfer food from a shared plate to your personal *kozara* (small dish), for example, is to use the opposite end of your chopsticks. However, you will often see groups of friends disregarding this. What isn't done is to rest your chopsticks on a communal dish, to pick through a shared dish for the morsels you want, or to scrape your chopsticks together to "smooth" them—this implies they are substandard.

When drinking from a shared bottle or *sake* flask, drinkers generally pour for one another, using both hands to show respect. This rule is almost always observed, at least for the first drink, and then depending on the company you are in, may be ignored. Some diners dislike such standing on ceremony. However, whenever drinks are being poured, it is universal practice for the recipient to show his or her gratitude by either lifting or simply gripping the glass or cup. Again, two hands are more respectful than one. This also goes for passing and receiving dishes etc.

If language is an issue for you, take heart in knowing that allowances will be made. The Japanese don't expect you to know all about their customs. A simple show of appreciation will take you far. You can express this by gentle body language, avoiding fussy ordering, or—if you have been treated especially well—offering to buy the master a beer toward the end of your visit.

In small, cramped establishments, be prepared to make room for extra customers. You may be asked to move seats. If confronted by aggressive patrons, don't show anger: it will only be seen as further disruption.

Ask for the check with the universal scribbling gesture, or by holding up two hands with your index fingers, making an "X." (This is also the sign for "no good," and you may encounter it if trying to enter an izakaya that is full, or has closed, or where the master feels unable to make you comfortable.) In many izakaya the check will be no more than a number on a sliver of paper. It is never quibbled over—unless there has been a serious mistake. It is standard practice to charge for the appetizer: about 500 yen per person.

14 oz. (400g) beef small intestine
2 oz. (60g) beef fourth stomach (Abomasum)
   * Substitutes could include tripe and beef chuck or round
2 oz. (60g) red miso, preferably from 100% soy beans
1 tbsp. coarse brown sugar
1 cup (240ml) ruby port wine
1 *bouquet garni* (celery, parsley and bay leaf) *see Step 2
1 bunch scallion or ½ *naganegi* white scallion, thinly sliced
4 large hard-boiled eggs, optional
Garlic toast *recipe below

"Motsu" Beef Intestine Stew

もつ煮込み
Motsu Nikomi

Not everyone with whom I've shared a meal here has leapt at the pros-
pect of eating intestines, but no one has emitted less than a moan of
intense pleasure upon tasting this rich and deep miso stew. The boiled
egg and garlic herb toast are perfect to mop it all up.

1. In a large pot, combine the beef organs and plenty
of water. Bring to a rapid boil and drain in a colander.
Return the organs to the pot and add water. Repeat boiling and draining a few times, skimming the scum from
the surface. In a colander, rinse the organs well under
running water.

2. Meanwhile, make a bouquet garni. Cut cheesecloth
into 6 in. (15cm) square, place celery stalk, parsley sprigs
and bay leaf in the center, wrap, and bind with string to
make a sachet.

3. Return the organs to the pot, add water to cover by 2
in. (5cm), and bring to a boil. Add the sugar, ruby port
and miso, and lower heat to a simmer. Add the boiled
eggs and stew for 2 hours, skimming the scum and fat as
necessary. More water should be added as the soup evap-
orates. Add the bouquet garni and simmer for 45 minutes.
Check taste. If it seems thin, thicken with more miso. If
too rich, add water and simmer a little longer.

4. Pour the stew into warmed shallow serving bowls
along with the boiled eggs, and top with the sliced scallions. Serve with slices of garlic toast.

Garlic Herb Toast

1 in. (2.5cm) thick slices of baguette

Garlic herb butter

8 tbsp. (4 oz./115g) unsalted butter, softened to room temperature	¼ tsp. minced fresh thyme
	1 tbsp. minced shallot
2 garlic cloves, minced	1 tsp. salt
1 tbsp. minced fresh parsley	A pinch of ground black pepper
¼ tsp. minced fresh basil	
¼ tsp. minced fresh rose-mary	

Mix all butter ingredients well with a rubber spatula.
Alternatively, put in a food processor and pulse for 20
seconds until well mixed. Cover and refrigerate to firm.
Cut baguette as required; toast the baguette slices and
spread with the butter while hot.

山利喜

CLOCKWISE FROM TOP: Peace and pleasure. The annex's second floor is generally packed by 6:30 p.m.; a cheerful regular at the counter; cellphone trinkets of the cartoon pig and a dish of offal stew, to mark Yamariki's 80th anniversary; East meets West—Yamada in Western chef's whites, with Japanese charcoal fan at the ready.

Shark Fin Aspic

This exotic jelly brings together classic French technique with Chinese and Japanese ingredients. You can buy shark's fin in cans or dried. Thoroughly rehydrate — some chefs do this over a period of days.   *Recipe p. 100*

Grilled Green Salad

To offset the hearty meat dishes, this quick-grilled salad brims with healthy fiber, chlorophyl and phytochemicals. The subtle dressing is of grapeseed oil, with pistachios and shallots.   *Recipe p. 100*

Littleneck Clam Broth with *Miso*

This is a dish you can really personalize. With the excellent range of miso pastes available in most major cities and online, enjoy blending rich red or lighter white and yellow miso for the flavor you prefer. The Japanese clams, called *asari*, are slightly different to littlenecks but close enough. Both produce a soup rich in *umami*.   *Recipe p. 101*

Grilled Whole *Surume* Squid

Great for outdoor barbecue (especially if your neighbors are over-sensitive to cooking smells). Grill slowly until crisp outside, and the texture is chewy. The smoky, powerful squid flavor, together with soy sauce and ginger, goes brilliantly with *sake*.   *Recipe p. 101*

Grilled Green Salad

焼野菜サラダ

Midori no Yaki Yasai Salada

P. 98

SERVES 4

8 oz. (230g) bunch spinach
8 oz. (230g) *mizuna* leaves

For grilling

⌈ 1 zucchini
1 small bell pepper or 2 Japanese *piman* peppers
2 mild green chili peppers such as Anaheim and Amanaga
4 oz. (115g) green beans
1 Japanese cucumber or ⅓ English cucumber, unpeeled
⌊ 4 medium asparagus spears

Dressing

⌈ 2 tbsp. white wine vinegar
2 tsp. minced shallot
¼ tsp. salt
⅛ tsp. freshly ground pepper
⌊ 6 tbsp. safflower oil

2 tbsp. chopped pistachios, toasted

1. Bring a large pot with salted water to a boil. Have ready ice water in a bowl. Cook spinach and mizuna separately, shock in ice water, drain and lightly squeeze out any excess water. Cut into 2 in. (5cm) lengths and set aside.
2. Combine the vinegar, shallots, salt and pepper in a small bowl. Gradually whisk in the oil to emulsify.
3. As required clean, seed and cut the vegetables for grilling. Grill over low flame.
4. Lay the boiled spinach and mizuna leaves on a serving plate. Arrange grilled vegetables, spoon the dressing over, and top with the toasted chopped pistachios.

Shark Fin Aspic

ふかひれの煮こごり

Fukahire no Nikogori

P. 98

MAKES 1 rectangular mold,
8×8×1½ in. (20×20×3cm)

7 oz. (200g) rehydrated and shredded shark fin
3 cups (720ml) *dashi* stock, room temperature *recipe p. 101
2 tsp. minced peel of *yuzu* citrus or lemon
2 tsp. yuzu juice
3 tbsp. soy sauce
1 tbsp. *sake*
1 tsp. salt
6 tbsp. (1½ oz./420mg) powdered gelatin
Kinome sprigs, optional

1. In a medium bowl, bloom the gelatin by sprinkling over ½ cup of the dashi stock. Set aside for 10 minutes.
2. In a small saucepan, add the remaining dashi, the shredded shark fin, yuzu juice, soy sauce, salt, and sake. Heat just to a boil then immediately remove from heat. Add the shark fin mixture and the minced citrus peel into the bloomed gelatin, and mix well (make sure the gelatin is completely dissolved).
3. Pour the mixture into the mold. Refrigerate until set, about 1–2 hours.
4. To unmold: Run a thin knife around the edge of aspic. Slice into 1-inch thick pieces. Arrange on a serving plate and garnish with kinome sprigs.

Disposable chopsticks are the norm, and while some izakaya set out decorative ceramic pieces to rest them on, others offer humble items such as a single peanut. And others still show that they think it's all too much fuss, in which case many patrons fashion their own from the chopstick envelope. Uber-polite diners wrap their used chopsticks in the envelope upon leaving, but most people don't bother.

Grilled Whole *Surume* Squid

するめいか姿焼き

Surumeika Sugata Yaki

MAKES 1 whole squid

P. 99

1 whole common (*surume*) squid
Sea salt
1 lemon wedge
2 teaspoons of grated ginger

1. To clean squid: pull and separate the tentacles and head from the body. Discard head. Trim the two longer tentacles to the same length as the others. Wash the tentacles well. Discard the innards, wash the body well under running cold water, and blot dry. Insert your hand into the body, remove the transparent cartilage and discard.
2. Salt the body and tentacles and broil on a medium charcoal or gas grill, flipping once, until cooked through, about 7–8 minutes. Cut the body into ¼ in. (1.25cm) thick rings. Arrange on a serving plate along with the lemon wedge and the grated ginger.

Littleneck Clam Broth with Miso

あさりの吸い物 味噌仕立て

Asari no Suimono Mizo Jitate

SERVES 4

P. 99

1 lb. (450g) small littleneck clams in shell
1¼ oz. (35g) *akadashi* miso
1¼ oz. (35g) white miso
3 cups (720ml) *dashi* stock *recipe at right

1. Cover the clams with salted water place for a few hours in a dark place to allow them to expel sand and grit. Scrub the shells thoroughly under cold running water.
2. In a medium pan, pour in the dashi stock and add the clams. Cook over medium-low heat. Just before the boil, dissolve akadashi miso and white miso, tasting as you do so. This soup should taste of clam broth, not miso.

DASHI

Dashi is the basis of Japanese soups, stews, stock concentrates and sauces, and the better your dashi, the more successful your meal will be. Powdered instant dashi is readily available, but it is simple to make your own—and avoid the additives often contained in those products. The more refined dashi uses *katsuo* bonito flakes, which are not cheap, but excellent results can be had with *niboshi* dried small sardines, or *ago* flying fish. These produce a smokier flavor, which may be just what you want, especially in soup noodle dishes.

To make about 1 qt. (1L) dashi stock: Heat 1qt (1L) water until tepid (86°F/30°C), then add in three 2×3 in. (5×7.5cm) strips of *kombu* kelp (about 0.7 oz/20g). Bring slowly to a simmer over 20-30 minutes. When simmering, immediately remove the kombu, skim the scum from the surface and bring to a boil. Add ¼ cup (60ml) of cold water to quell the bubbles and immediately lower the heat. Add in 2 oz. (60g) bonito flakes. When all bonito flakes have soaked up the liquid and the liquid has barely returned to the boil, turn off the heat. Leave for five minutes and strain through a sieve lined with a fine cloth, or a large coffee filter. Cool at room temperature without covering.

The *katsu-bako*, a plane for shaving the dried bonito into flakes.

MIXERS AND ELIXIRS
IZAKAYA DRINKING

What I love about izakaya is that they accord equal weight to food and drink, unlike the average restaurant or bar, which favors one over the other. It is accepted and even expected that you will arrive with a thirst as good as your appetite. At the same time, no one will look askance—even at the most gourmet izakaya—if your chief aim is to have a few drinks (though naturally you will order a small something to soak up the alcohol).

Thanks to most izakaya offering a vast variety of regional *sake* and *shochu*, beer, and sometimes wine, you can be as adventurous in your drinking as in how you navigate the food menu. Nor are teetotalers neglected: there is always iced *oolong* tea, hot green tea, and other drinks.

Most customers begin with a **beer**, or *biiru*—friends of mine who don't even like the stuff do so too. They say beer "refreshes" the throat for what is to come. The preliminary beer is also a way for everyone to kick off the evening on the same note, and it buys you time to consider what to order, and what to drink with it.

All izakaya offer draft, or *nama*, beer, invariably from one of the major breweries, but the quality will vary in direct proportion to the izakaya's overall prices, and it is safe to say that the budget izakaya takes no special pride in its beer or serving equipment. Draft beer comes either in glasses or, at cheaper places, glass mugs called *jokki*, which will be medium (*chu jokki*) or large (*dai jokki*), holding well over a pint—enough to go quite flat by the time many drinkers get to the bottom. Unless I know the draft at an izakaya is especially worthwhile, I generally go for bottled, or *bin*, beer.

"**Sake**," pronounced with a short "e" as in "get," and also honorifically called *o-sake*, is the generic word for any kind of alcohol. It also refers specifically to the brewed rice beverage *nihon shu*, "Japanese alcohol." It is often translated as "rice wine," but this is a misnomer since sake is brewed in a manner more like beer. Sake is often served in a ceramic flask, or *tokkuri*, from which you fill small porcelain or clay cups (*o-choko*). I like the small, frequent sips that this drinking style encourages. Sake may also be poured straight into a glass, which may be placed on a saucer or in a *masu*, a small wooden box made of Japanese cypress. The server might show his or her generosity by over-pouring, so that the surplus sake floods the box.

Sake can be drunk at any temperature between chilled (*reishu*) and hot (*atsu kan*)—the izakaya Saiki (see p. 50) even serves a semi-frozen, sherbet-like brew, though the master concedes mischievously that this is not something he does to his good sake! Serious drinkers of sake generally prefer it slightly warmed: a state called *nuru kan*, or at room temperature (*jo-on*). But the ideal temperature depends on the type of sake being served and, of course, your preference.

Many izakaya and bars sculpt their ice by hand. It is delivered in large blocks by specialists, is made from pure water and is extremely hard, so you can sip slowly without your drink turning watery.

Sake's alcohol content is around 15 percent, and it has numerous official designations: that which is made only from rice is known as *junmai shu*, literally "pure rice sake," and sake made with a small amount of alcohol added during the brewing process is *honjozo shu*. This is a legitimate technique to bring out flavor, and not related to the mass-production practice of adding large quantities of alcohol simply to increase output. Prestigious awards for honjozo sake prove that it can be every bit as superb as junmai.

The most expensive sake tend to be either *ginjo* or *daiginjo* styles, which use rice whose grain has been milled to at least 40 or 50 percent respectively of its original size. Since the all-important starch in sake rice is concentrated in the center of the grain, these sake are seen as more refined. But again, the most delicious sake is simply the one you like best.

Sake is typically pasteurized, but you will find *nama* or "raw" unpasteurized sake, which I like for its fresh taste; *nigori*, or unfiltered sake, with a cloudy appearance and sometimes a slight fizz; aged sake, or *koshu* (most sake does not keep well and should be consumed soon after opening); and the undiluted *genshu*, with an alcohol content of around 20 percent, which you can enjoy on the rocks. Sake's flavors and aromas are as infinite as wine's, so you are bound to find one that suits you. Most izakaya staff will be happy to introduce you to a variety. Just say *o-susume wo kudasai*: "please give me your recommendation."

Here's a big irony: despite being seen as the national drink, sake is unpopular in Japan. By 2007, domestic sales as a percentage of the national alcohol market had plummeted to single digits. There are many possible reasons for this: it is often said that sake has developed an image problem, being seen as the drink of old men (at which I take offence). Also behind its decline may be the increase in sales of wine and cheap, low-malt beer, while distilled shochu spirit has enjoyed a huge spike in popularity.

Once seen as the poor man's sake, "**shochu**" began its renaissance in 2003—outselling sake for the first time in over a half-century—when young women caught on to its purported health benefits. These range from preventing heart attack and stroke, to helping you stay slim, and even being hangover-free. It is true that shochu contains far fewer calories than sake, beer or wine, and that it has been found to boost the enzymes that prevent blood clots. As for the latter claim . . . after much dedicated field-testing, I can assure you it is false!

Shochu can be distilled from almost any plant or grain but is most commonly made from barley, sweet potatoes, or sugar. It comes in two main types: multiple distilled and single distilled, with the former being pretty much taste-

A barrel, or *taru*, of Ryozeki *sake* at Shinsuke. The barrel is made from Japanese cedar, which adds fragrance and a mild natural preservative to its contents. Barrel sake must be drunk fresh and is not shipped in summer, when temperatures are too high.

less and odorless, making it ideal for mixing into easy-drinking cocktails—and of no interest on its own. Single-distilled shochu retains the flavor of its key ingredient, with barley shochu (*mugi-jochu*) being mild and fragrant, and the sweet potato variety—*imo-jochu*—exhibiting a powerful, earthy flavor that you either love or hate. Shochu distilleries, mostly concentrated in southern Japan around Kyushu, take great pride in their regional differences, and the thousands of different styles are absolutely worth exploring.

Shochu's alcohol content is around 25 percent, though some styles exceed 40 percent. There are countless ways to drink it: straight up, on the rocks (I like it this way), as a mixed drink, or diluted with cold or hot water (see glossary p. 154 for shochu cocktails). Given its pungency, imo jochu does not mix well with anything but water. I find it delicious diluted with hot water.

At Maru, three sweet-potato *shochu*. At left is Hachiman; center is Sato Black; right is Kichohozan. Hachiman is a bracing "white mold" (*shiro-koji*) style. The latter two are made from black rice mold (*kuro-koji*)—generally producing a richer drink. Being distilled, shochu keeps indefinitely, unlike *sake*.

If shochu's supposed health benefits spurred its sales to go ballistic, this had a precedent: in the mid-1990s, a media frenzy over the beneficial effects of polyphenols kick-started a transformation of Japan's **wine** market. "Sommelier" became a household word (there was even a comic book and TV series of this name) and increasing numbers of izakaya began offering wine. The good news for wine fans is that the fad hasn't abated (which I guess makes it not a fad), and at more upmarket izakaya particularly, you should be well served.

There's little that excites the Japanese consumer more than a product boom, and with almost every food or drink trend, women have led the way. I would also argue that women have changed izakaya culture by contributing a calming influence, and while the staggering, red-faced salaryman at such raucous, male-dominated districts as Shimbashi, near Ginza, remains perennial, the general tone of izakaya is now more civilized than it was two decades ago. Of course obnoxious drunkenness happens— there is one ritual called *iki iki* drinking (essentially a sculling contest) partaken of by young males—which will put you off your food. But in my experience, and at the sort of izakaya I have included in this book, it is rare.

Finally, if visiting izakaya around year's end, you will almost certainly encounter a rowdy office-worker gathering known as the *bonenkai*, or literally, "forget the year party." New Year's parties will be much the same, and while generally benign, they generate a hell of a noise. Check your seating arrangements carefully if you're looking for an intimate evening. Alternatively, you may decide to join in. *Kanpai* (Cheers)!

TRADITIONAL
RADICAL

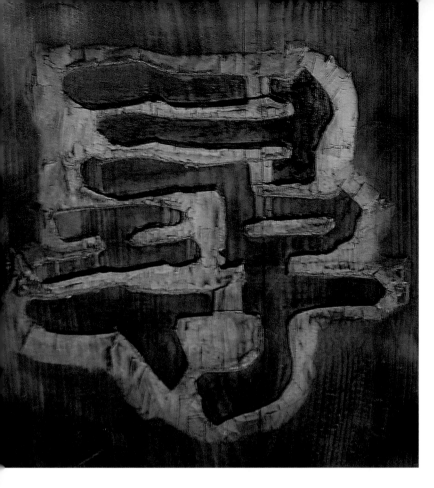

尋 Hiro

I arrive at Hiro, a tiny izakaya squeezed under the railway arches in Nakameguro, south-western Tokyo, in my usual state of hungry anticipation over what the young master, Kuniharu Takahashi, has posted for the evening on his blackboard menu. Hiro is Takahashi's first izakaya—he hung out his *noren* curtain in 2004—but after a fifteen-year background in the kitchens of a Japanese caterer and a lunchbox maker, followed by long stints in high-end Chinese and European restaurants, he brings to his business both the Japanese culinary basics and a broad understanding of ingredients and cuisines. His eye for unusual seasonal items and his intuition for fresh juxtapositions have earned him a loyal following.

But tonight, ducking under the blue shop curtain and expecting to find the place crowded, I'm torn between feeling glad and disappointed. Straight away I see that I am the only customer. Takahashi is seated behind the counter, working on something in a stainless steel bowl. He rises slightly and issues the standard "*Irasshaimase!*" greeting. I take a stool in front of him, order a beer and, to break the ice, understate the obvious: "A bit quiet," I say.

Takahashi grins. It is 9:30 p.m. and he has been open for two hours. "You're my first customer," he says, unfazed, and sets about preparing the *otoshi* appetizer. At Hiro, this may be any of a range of original homemade morsels, such as thin wedges of *daikon* peel pickled in garlic and soy sauce, or a gelatinous, salty egg yolk preserved in miso paste, or perhaps a dish of grated *tororo* mountain yam sprinkled with *aonori* powdered seaweed, and served with *wasabi*.

AS I STUDY the blackboard menu I think about the tenuous existence of the small izakaya. It might appear to be doing well—if you visit when it is crowded—but because of its size, will never achieve more than minimal sales and in weathering the inevitable lulls, must bear the cost of wasted ingredients. This is especially an expense to be considered in Japanese cuisine, where freshness is paramount, and calls for shrewd shopping at the market and a variety of techniques to produce tasty dishes from components that, although only a hair's breadth past their absolute prime, can no longer be served raw. There are many ways of treating fish to extend its shelf-life, for example, such as pressing it with *kombu* seaweed with a hint of vinegar to preserve it or, as in the dish *ichiyaboshi*, by drying butterflied whole fish overnight, or even flouring and deep frying it to make a cold vinegared salad such as *nanban zuke*.

When I arrive, Takahashi is preparing tiny *hotaru ika* baby firefly squid, a spring specialty traditionally eaten as sashimi with a sweet *su-miso* white-miso/vinegar dressing. With precision he picks up each squid from the steel bowl and with a pair of boning tweezers removes its eyes and beak before transferring it to another bowl. I ask what he is doing, as I've never seen it done. He explains, adding, "Many chefs don't bother. But it takes

out the bitterness and hard texture of these organs." He hands me one of the little purple molluscs. It is barely the size of my thumb, with miniature tentacles, and though not even a mouthful, it is indeed delicious. Takahashi serves it not with the ubiquitous su-miso dressing (which he dislikes), but with a mixture of soy sauce, hot Japanese *karashi* mustard, and *ishiru* sauce, the equivalent of Thai *nam pla* fish sauce.

Takahashi's preference for this unusual pairing is typical of his adventurous palate. Similarly, he serves sashimi of *katsuo*—rich, blood-red bonito—not with the traditional condiments of soy sauce and grated ginger or minced garlic, but with karashi mustard and soy sauce, something which other izakaya masters to whom I mentioned this regarded with incredulity (though having tried it, I would say that it works). At the Tsukiji fish market, Takahashi chooses fish for sashimi that are almost exclusively used by other chefs only for cooking, such as *hokke*, an inexpensive grilling fish from Hokkaido, generally supplied frozen, but which at its peak of freshness is deliciously creamy when eaten raw. He also makes a salad of *nanohana* rapini leaves and *wakame* seaweed, dressed with vinegar, soy and wasabi, and topped with roasted sesame seeds. Again, nanohana in Japan is almost never eaten raw, being considered too bitter, but the roundness of Takahashi's dressing pulls the combination together.

Of course, experimentation has its price. "I have a lot of successes—and failures," he says. "I'll buy an ingredient I've never seen before, then think . . . what can I do with this? Sometimes I'll buy some unusual fish for sashimi and then realise you can't eat it raw. But if there's something I don't know, I'll buy it."

Much of Takahashi's cooking defies convention, but this should come as no surprise, for the only thing he ever wanted to do was to cook. He arrived in Tokyo from the northern prefecture of Gunma at the age of nineteen, and soon landed his first serious kitchen job.

"It was tough at first, learning knife technique and so on, but I tried pretty hard," he says. "I was never averse to work, since I knew that I would be in the kitchen for the same hours no matter what. I decided that if I worked seriously I would get things done quickly, quicker than other people, and I could be the best, wherever I worked." He speaks with a refreshing frankness and no false modesty. "When I was at the European restaurants I became the top, I was top at the bento store, I didn't reach the top at the Chinese place, but I reached the position where things would be left up to me," he says.

He admits that this stage of his learning was about technique above all, and it was not until much later that he glimpsed the big picture that would mold his career. "When I was younger it was all about working fast, cutting fast, cutting cleanly, and all my emphasis was on preparation," he says. "But it wasn't until I was about thirty that I truly understood what cooking was about. When I finally understood seasoning, it was—*ahaa!*—a revelation. I had wanted to do my own place when I was about twenty-six, but looking back it's good that I didn't because, to tell the truth, I had no idea what I was doing."

THIS MELDING OF chutzpah and humility strikes me as the healthiest expression of Japanese-style self-confidence, and despite Takahashi's menu featuring dishes such as tomato cream pasta (a holdover from his restaurant days), the food at Hiro is overwhelmingly native. One perennial dish, and something you will find on izakaya menus everywhere, is "Sliced Tomato." It is simply that: a sliced tomato, served with a small mound of sea salt and sometimes mayonnaise, and dates from a time when tomatoes were exotic produce in Japan. Takahashi's tomato, however, is a brix 9—measured on the universal sweetness scale that reads only around 3.5 for your average supermarket tomato—and is the firmest, sweetest tomato I have eaten. I tell him I am glad to see him continuing the Sliced Tomato tradition, and he answers with a lesson in the fundamentals of Japanese cooking.

"If something is tasty without having anything done to it, it is better not to do anything," he says. "Don't be excessive. Of course there are many variables and you adjust spices, condiments, add salt or soy sauce and so on, but as much as possible, you try not to tamper. That's the basis of Japanese food—not addition, but subtraction. Just remove any bad smell or bitterness, and serve. Though while I'm cooking, I might add a little something to make it that *little bit more* tasty."

My solo evening at Hiro's counter pays off (for me if not for him). Takahashi offers me to try—along with his firefly squid—a spicy soy sauce from a plastic container that he has loaded with whole green chilis and kept for two years; a tofu fermented with miso—also for two years—and which tastes like the richest blue cheese; and a glass of turtle blood wine mixed with apple juice (by reservation, he also serves turtle hotpots).

I wonder if a chef of his curiosity and knowledge might be better off making *kaiseki* Japanese haute cuisine, in which big budgets

Chicken and Vegetable *"Nanban"* Escabeche

This national favorite probably derives from the 16th century Portuguese settlers of southern Japan, who brought with them deep frying—i.e. *tempura*—and this dish, which in Japanese means "chicken and vegetables southern-barbarian marinade." Hardly a politically correct name, though barely offensive today. A bit like *pasta alla puttanesca*, I suppose. You can also make a delicious *aji* nanban with whole small horse mackerel, battered and deep fried. The only vegetable required is thinly sliced onion, and the essential dried chili. *Recipe p. 112*

allow chefs virtual free reign. But I know the answer before I have finished asking. With his long hair, Levis, low-slung apron, and late opening hours, Takahashi's preference is for izakaya. He dislikes the formality of high level Japanese dining. "I want to run the sort of place where you can eat almost anything, drink as much as you like, and truly relax," he says, gesturing along his small counter which seats only twelve. "And where I can tell an annoying customer, 'What the hell are you crapping on about!?'"

Like most of its neighbors along this nightlife strip, Hiro is charmingly run down. Inside,

it is defiantly austere. The naked hanging lightbulbs seem to quiver as trains rumble above, and the bare, L-shaped counter fronts a dim, open kitchen merely an arm span wide. But if there is a reason why the décor takes second place, tonight I have uncovered it and it is Takahashi's unwavering dedication to food.

During my research for this chapter, Takahashi took on an apprentice—the first assistant he has had—and began making plans to move to bigger and brighter premises, as the under-the-tracks oasis of Nakameguro's many izakaya was set to fall, like so much of Tokyo, to a developer's wrecking ball.

Nanohana Rabe and *Wakame* Seaweed Salad

This dish displays Takahashi's love of contrasting textures, with smooth *wakame*, mildly crisp *nanohona*, a light oil dressing and pinches of crunchy toasted sesame. Nanohana, served in this photograph with its flowers, is a soft-leafed, slightly bitter green. If you cannot obtain nanohana, or very tender brocolli rabe, substitute according to the recipe. *Recipe p. 112*

Chicken and Vegetable "*Nanban*" Escabeche

鶏と野菜の南蛮漬け

Tori to Yasai no Nanban-zuke

P. 110

SERVES 6

1 half boneless chicken
  breast, without skin,
  5 to 6 oz. (140–170g)
4 tbsp. soy sauce
1 tbsp. *sake*

All-purpose flour for dusting
  chicken
Vegetable oil
White sesame seeds,
  toasted

Vegetables
- 1 small bell pepper
- 1 celery stalk
- ½ small onion
- 1 Japanese cucumber, unpeeled
- 1 small carrot

Marinade
- 1 cup (240ml) *dashi* stock *recipe p. 101
- ⅔ cup (160ml) rice vinegar
- 6 tbsp. soy sauce
- 6 tbsp. *mirin*
- 4 tsp. red chili pepper flakes

1. Cut the chicken breast into bite-size pieces. In a small bowl, combine soy sauce and sake. Add the chicken breast and refrigerate, turning from time to time, for at least 20 minutes.

2. Cut all vegetables into ¼ in. (6mm) strips or oblique pieces. Set aside.

3. For the marinade: mix all marinade ingredients in a small saucepan and bring to a simmer to evaporate the alcohol. Immediately remove from heat and keep warm.

4. Remove the chicken pieces from the refrigerator and lightly dry with paper towel. Dust with the flour. In a medium frying pan with at least 2 in. sides, heat ¾ in. (about 2cm) of the oil to 360°C (180°C). Fry the chicken pieces, flipping once, until golden and crispy.

5. In a kettle or small saucepan, bring water to boil. Place the fried chicken pieces in a sieve and pour the boiling water over the chicken to drain excess oil.

6. Place the chicken and the vegetables in a shallow flat container such as a Pyrex square dish, and pour the warm marinade sauce over all. Let cool a little at room temperature. Cover with plastic wrap and marinate in refrigerator overnight.

7. Arrange the chicken and vegetables on serving dishes and spoon over the marinade sauce. Sprinkle with the toasted sesame seeds.

Nanohana Rabe and *Wakame* Seaweed Salad

菜の花とわかめのサラダ

Nanohana to Wakame no Salada

P. 111

SERVES 4

1 lb. (450g) broccoli rabe
  * Other bitter salad leaves can be substituted such as Belgian endive, radicchio, *nanohana* rabe, or frisee
1 vine-ripened tomato
1 oz. (30g) salted or 6g dried *wakame* seaweed, reconstituted

Dressing
- 3 tbsp. vegetable oil
- 1 tbsp. rice vinegar
- ½ tbsp. soy sauce
- 1 tbsp. *mirin*
- ¼ tsp. minced garlic

- 1 tsp. *nam pla* (Thai fish sauce)
- 1 tsp. fresh lemon juice
- ⅛ tsp. grated wasabi

1 tbsp. sesame seeds, toasted
2 tbsp. finely sliced scallions
Salt

1. Wash the salad greens in several changes of cold water and spin dry. Cut into bite-sized pieces. Cut the tomato into quarters, seed and roughly chop into large dices. Cover the salad greens and tomatoes separately with damp paper towels and chill in refrigerator.

2. If using salted wakame, soak in cold water to remove saltiness for 3–5 minutes. For dried wakame, rehydrate according to instructions on the package. (Some cooks like to blanch after soaking to achieve a greener color. However don't soak or blanch too long, or the wakame will turn jelly-like.) Lightly squeeze water from the wakame, neatly fold and cut into bite-size pieces. Trim and discard any tough parts, such as the frond spines.

3. Cut the wakame into bite-size pieces.

4. In a small bowl, whisk all dressing ingredients. Set aside.

5. In a medium bowl, place the salad greens and toss with some of the dressing to taste. Gently toss in the wakame and tomatoes, and arrange in a serving bowl. Sprinkle with scallions and sesame seeds.

BORN HUNGRY

At the peak of the global celebrity-chef craze, a Japanese friend told me he was grateful to the British kitchen-whizz Jamie Oliver, for "making cooking fun." "When I'm chopping an onion nowadays," he said, "I can feel like a rock star." I puzzled at this, since Japanese chefs—with their pride in workmanship, deft technique and knowledge of ingredients—are already figures to revere. The answer may be that their brilliant work is taken for granted, since from childhood the Japanese are inculcated with their food culture. Culinary education is transmitted in large part through a plethora of food-obsessed TV shows, cuisine-themed *anime* cartoons, and culinary *manga* comic books. Here are six food-media icons:

■ *Anpan-man*: Children's manga and anime character created in 1968, Anpan-man is a rosy-cheeked super hero whose round head is in fact a bun filled with sweet bean jam. He battles such villains as Baikin-man ("Mr. Bacteria"), and takes pity on the hungry by giving them chunks of his head to eat. When he loses his head, a friendly baker, "Uncle Jam," makes him another. Other characters include "Butter Girl," "Mr. Sliced Bread," and the dog, "Cheese."

■ *Sazae-san*: Comic strip and anime that debuted in 1946 featuring the innocent adventures of a young housewife, Sazae-san, and her extended family. The action centers on home life, often around the dinner table. Many character names are seafood-related (*sazae* is a turban shell) and include salmon roe, trout, skipjack tuna, seaweed, cod, and blowfish. *Sazae-san* is the second-longest running TV series in history.

■ *Mr. Ajikko* ("Mr. Taste-guy"): A manga and anime in which a cooking-obsessed schoolboy does battle with master chefs. The animated series, which ran to one hundred episodes, was created by Yasuhiro Imagawa, director of *Mobile Fighter G Gundam*. The manga inspired the blockbuster *Iron Chef* TV show.

■ *Oishinbo* ("The Gourmet"): Enormously popular semi-educational manga featuring the adventures of a food-savvy journalist who takes issue with how food is served in every restaurant he visits, and works to set things right. The manga has sold over 100 million copies, and has inspired TV dramas, anime and cookbooks.

© Tetsu Kariya/Akira Hanasaku/Shogakukan Big Comic Spirits

■ *The Sommelier*: Manga and later a soap opera that appeared with Japan's wine boom. The half-Japanese, half-French hero travels the world to relocate the wine his mother introduced him to when she was alive. The viewer adventures with him, learning not only about wines and different countries, but the importance of wine service.

■ *Natsuko no Sake*: Manga in which a young girl takes over the family brewery after her brother's death, and commits to making the best *sake* from rice established by her brother. The story patriotically stresses the importance of rice culture. Its launch in 1988 coincided with the *jizake* boom in regional sake.

Omelet with Semi-dried Baby Sardines

A straightforward, truly comforting dish that works best when the omelet's insides are steaming hot and runny. Substitute crab for the semi-dried sardines. Eat with a dash of soy sauce over the grated *daikon* radish.   *Recipe p. 116*

Soy Marinated *Daikon* Peels

This crunchy, salty-sour appetizer is extremely moreish with a drink, and a perfect use for the daikon peel you might normally discard. It takes around a week to mature, but if refrigerated and covered in its marinade, will keep indefinitely in a sealed container. Lay plastic wrap over the peels to maintain moisture. *Recipe p. 116*

Fried *Udon* Noodles

What I like about Takahashi's cooking is his speed and lack of snobbery. This dish is dead-easy: all ingredients are store-bought (noodles, red ginger, *surimi* etc.) and combined in minutes. The secret behind its solid, reassuring flavor, he says, is a teaspoonful of lard. *Recipe p. 117*

Miso-cured Tofu

This hors d'oeuvre takes the concept of "slow food" to a new level. Leave it for two years—yes, *years*—and you'll have a stunning blue-cheese-like delicacy to spread on crackers, and to eat with wine, *sake*, olives, or pickles. (You can also eat it after two days—see recipe.) *Recipe p. 117*

Omelet with Semi-dried Baby Sardines

しらす玉子焼き

Shirasu Tamago-yaki

P. 114

SERVES 2

2 large whole eggs
1 tbsp. *shirasuboshi* semi-dried baby sardines
1 tbsp. chopped scallion
1 tbsp. grated *daikon* radish
1 tbsp. vegetable oil
Freshly ground black pepper to taste
Salt

1. Taste test the baby sardines for saltiness before mixing with the eggs (if not salty, add salt to the egg mixture. If very salty, reduce the amount used). In a medium bowl, beat the eggs and mix in the baby sardines, scallion and ground pepper.
2. Heat the oil until distributed evenly over the bottom of an 8 in. (20cm) non-stick frying pan over medium-high heat. Pour in the egg mixture. With a rubber spatula, scramble the eggs using small, circular scribbling motions, for about 20 seconds. Spread the mixture evenly, jiggling the pan so that the runny parts flow between the creamy curds, and cook to your liking. If the egg seems to be cooking too quickly, remove from heat as needed. With the rubber spatula, roll the omelet into thirds, lifting one-third of the omelet from the top of the pan toward the center, and invert the omelet onto a warm serving plate to make the second fold. Serve with a dab of grated daikon radish.

Soy Marinated *Daikon* Peels

大根皮のしょうゆ漬け

Daikongawa no Shoyu-zuke

P. 115

MAKES ½ cup

⅛ in. (3mm) thick daikon radish peels from 2 rounds of daikon, each 1½ in. (4cm) thick
  * see peeling methods in Step 1. You can use the peeled daikon for such dishes as Simmered Daikon with Pork and Miso Sauce (p. 20)

Marinade

1 tbsp. soy sauce	⅛ tsp. chili flakes
½ tbsp. rice vinegar	1 small clove garlic, crushed
¼ tbsp. *mirin*	
¼ tbsp. water, more to taste	

1. To peel daikon (*katsura-muki* technique): Wash daikon rounds well. Hold a daikon round away from you in one hand, and using a long thin knife (such as an *usuba* knife, without a bolster) move the blade backward and forward while rotating the radish towards blade. Peel a thickness of around ¼ in. (6mm). Alternatively, on a chopping board, cut the skin into ¼ in. (6mm) thickness with a regular knife, trying to cut peels as large as possible. Cut the peels into pieces, about ½×1½ in. (1.25×4cm).
2. In a container (preferably glass to prevent absorption of odors), mix all ingredients of the marinade together with the daikon radish peels. Marinate in refrigerator for about a week.

It is hardly suprising that izakaya feature in *manga* comic books, given the social interaction they facilitate. Above, Hiro master Takahashi (pictured opposite, enjoying a well-deserved beer), is shown on the left preparing a customer's drink. The manga artist told him he wanted to depict a place that was "run down."
© Shunju Aono/Shogakukan IKKI

Miso-cured Tofu

豆腐みそ漬け

Tofu Miso-zuke

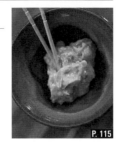

`MAKES` ¼ cup

P. 115

½ block extra firm tofu, about 6 oz. (170g)
½ cup (5 oz./145g) yellow *miso*
1 tsp. granulated sugar
1 tsp. *sake*

1. Wrap the tofu in a clean, non-terrycloth kitchen towel or paper towel, and place in a flat-bottomed dish with sides, such as a Pyrex square glass dish. Place a light weight such as another flat dish on top, and leave about 30 minutes to drain excess moisture.
2. In a medium bowl, combine miso, sugar and sake.
3. Line a small flat-bottomed container with three layers of paper towels. Spread the miso mixture on the paper towels, to ⅛ in. (3mm) thick and about the same dimensions as the tofu block, and place the tofu on top. Smear more miso all over the tofu, tightly seal with plastic wrap and place in refrigerator.
4. Change the plastic wrap and paper towels once a month and cure for a year or two until a texture of matured cheese is achieved. You don't have to wait this long—you can also enjoy firm, lightly cured tofu in about two days.

Fried *Udon* Noodles

焼きうどん

Yaki Udon

`SERVES` 4–5

P. 115

About 1 lb. (450g) *udon* noodles
2–3 tbsp. *Kaeshi* concentrate *recipe below
2 tsp. vegetable oil
1 tsp. pork lard or vegetable oil
8 *naruto* surimi slices, or thin slices of 2 surimi sticks
2 pinches bonito flakes (*katsuo kezuri-bushi*)
A handful thinly julienned *nori* seaweed
Store-bought pickled ginger (*benishoga*)

1. Have ready cold water in a large bowl and a colander in the sink. In a large pot of boiling water, cook the udon for about 1 minute less than the time indicated on package. Drain in the colander and transfer to the large bowl. Lightly rub and rinse the noodles under running cold water to stop cooking and remove excess starch.
2. In a large bowl, mix the cooked noodles and kaeshi concentrate. Toss well.
3. Fry the noodles in two batches: in a large non-stick frying pan, heat 1 tsp. of the oil over medium high heat. Add half of the noodles and sauté until the soy sauce is fragrant, about 1 minute. Add ½ tsp. of lard, 4 surimi slices and a pinch of bonito flakes. Toss well and season with salt and pepper to taste; fry the rest of the udon noodle in a same manner.
4. Place the fried udon noodles on a plate and top with the nori seaweed and pickled ginger.

Kaeshi Concentrate

`MAKES` about ½ cup

⌈ 4 tbsp. soy sauce
  4 tbsp. *mirin*
  A handful bonito flakes
⌊ Dried *kombu* kelp, about 1 in. (2.5cm) square

In a container with a lid, combine all ingredients and refrigerate for at least for three days. Will keep up to 3 months. Strain before use.

Grilled Chicken Breast with *Ume* Plum Paste

Sweet and tender chicken breast and sour *umeboshi* plums are a common pairing in Japanese cuisine; chopped *shiso* leaves make for a holy trinity. Here the (very fresh) chicken is cooked rare. Crushed umeboshi, called *bainiku*, is available in plastic squeeze-bottles. *Recipe p. 120*

Deep-fried Tofu with Mushroom Sauce

Atsu-age deep-fried tofu can be bought ready-made, but preparing it yourself is simple and the difference in taste and the crispness of the outer crust will amaze you. Takahashi's rich mushroom sauce is surprisingly easy to make.   *Recipe p. 120*

Spaghetti *con Vongole* in Japanese Style

In its own way, every noodle-loving nation embraces spaghetti. This popular dish may inspire you to invent others. Japanese spaghetti sauce ingredients commonly include *mentaiko* spicy cod roe, *maitake* and other mushrooms, *natto* fermented soybeans, *dashi*, *sake*, *umeboshi*, *shiso*, and *nori* seaweed.   *Recipe p. 121*

119

Grilled Chicken Breast with *Ume* Plum Paste

鶏肉の梅焼

Tori no Ume-yaki

SERVES 4

P. 118

2 small chicken breast halves, boneless and skinless
½ cup (120ml) soy sauce
2 tbsp. *umeboshi* plum paste (*bainiku*)
1 *shiso* leaf, chopped

1. Slice the chicken breasts on the diagonal into ¼ in. thick (6mm) thick pieces.
2. Heat a large heavy skillet over high heat. Briefly soak the chicken slices in a small bowl with soy sauce, then grill the chicken slices in the skillet until cooked while the center remains moist.
3. Arrange the chicken slices on a serving plate, smear with the *umeboshi* plum paste and sprinkle with chopped shiso.

Deep-fried Tofu with Mushroom Sauce

自家製厚揚げ きのこあん

Jikasei Atsu-age, Kinoko-an

SERVES 4

P. 119

1 block firm tofu, about 12½ oz. (350g)
4 tbsp. grated *daikon* radish
2 tsp. grated ginger
4 tsp. sliced scallion
Mild peppers, such as Anaheim or *shishito*, pierced and deep fried (optional)

Mushroom Sauce

1 cup (240ml) *dashi* stock *recipe p. 101
3 tbsp *mirin*
1 tbsp soy sauce
½ cup (120ml) mixed mushrooms, such as *shimeji*, *maitake*, julienned *shiitake*
1 tsp. potato starch, dissolved in 1 tsp. water

1. Wrap the tofu in a clean, non-terrycloth kitchen towel or paper towel, and place in a flat-bottomed dish with sides, such as a Pyrex square glass dish. Place a light weight such as another flat dish on top, and leave about 30 minutes to drain excess moisture. Wipe any moisture from the surface of the tofu and slice into 2×2×¾ in. (5×5×2cm) thick cakes. Set aside on a paper-lined dish.
2. In a heavy large pot, heat the oil to 360°F (180°C) and carefully slip the tofu cakes into the oil. Deep fry until golden-brown, about 2–3 minutes.
3. In a medium pot, combine the dashi, soy sauce, mirin, and mushrooms and bring to a boil. Immediately lower heat and pour in the potato starch slurry to thicken the sauce (don't boil the sauce again, or it will break up).
4. Place the tofu cakes in serving bowls, ladle the sauce over, and top with the grated daikon and ginger. Garnish with the fried peppers.

Spaghetti *con Vongole* in Japanese Style

あさりとしめじの和風パスタ
Asari to Shimeji no Wafu Pasuta

SERVES 4–5

P. 119

1 lb. (450g) littleneck clams (or steamer or vongole) in shell
1 lb. (450g) dry spaghetti
1 large clove garlic, sliced
1 seeded dried red chili or ½ teaspoon chili flakes
½ lb. (230g) *shimeji* mushrooms, or fresh *shiitake*
1 tbsp. vegetable oil
2 tsp. *sake*
1 tsp. or more soy sauce
A handful julienned *nori* seaweed
2 tbsp. thinly sliced scallions
Salt

1. In a medium bowl (preferably with a sieve insert), cover the clams with about 3 percent salted water. Place the bowl in a cool dark place for 2–3 hours to allow them to expel sand and dirt. Wash under running cold water, gently scrubbing shells clean.

2. In a large pot with salted boiling water, cook the spaghetti until tender yet *al dente.*

3. Meanwhile, heat the oil over low heat in a large frying pan. Add the sliced garlic and chili pepper and cook until fragrant, at least 5 minutes. When the garlic slices are turning golden, add the mushrooms and clams and stir. Pour in sake, cover the pan with a lid, and cook the clams until open, about 5 to 6 minutes. Discard any clams that do not open. Season with soy sauce and stir. Turn the heat to high, add in the cooked spaghetti and stir.

4. Arrange on serving plates and sprinkle with the nori seaweed and scallions.

LOVE OF
THE GAME

Morimoto

Yakitori barbecued chicken, essentially no more than pieces of cut chicken and other ingredients threaded on skewers and then grilled, is one of Japan's simplest dishes. But if you think turning out consistently good yakitori is child's play, you would be wrong. The freshness of the ingredients, their preparation, even the quality of the charcoal all affect the result, and the serious yakitori chef takes as much pride in his work as any skilled craftsman. I learned this watching the kitchen crew at Morimoto, the famed yakitori pub in the jam-packed shopping district of Shibuya.

From 9 a.m., store master Kuniyoshi Watanabe and his three morning staff are hard at work prepping, after closing their store at around 11 p.m. the night before. This is their routine, six days a week. The wood-veneered room is bright with fluorescent light. Upended stools stand on some of the log benches and the counter bristles with styrofoam boxes of produce. The men work with constant, fluid method from one task to the next, always cleaning as they go. Their selection of knives is amazing, from stubby paring knives to willowy sashimi blades, most of them handed down by past masters and so worn from decades of sharpening that they have assumed weird, dagger-like shapes.

The eel blade—Morimoto also serves grilled

eels—is especially unusual, the flat of one side being beveled somewhat like a chisel, to get under the eel's odd-shaped backbone. Eels are the first task for the master, who is behind the counter instructing an assistant in the art of filleting them live.

THERE ARE ONLY two tables at Morimoto, and at the second of these, against the far wall, an apprentice is preparing chicken skin. Almost six pounds of it arrive in a big plastic bag, like so many wet, white rags. The skin must be separated and sorted, cut into rectangles, stacked, sliced into thin strips, and threaded onto skewers. It is by far the most monotonous and painstaking job here: one strip of skin must be doubled over and pierced three or four times before being pushed down the skewer. The multiple actions yield a bunched morsel only a quarter-inch thick, and must be repeated until the six-inch skewer is full with a consistent volume. It will take three hours to produce fifty skewers of skin which, when the orders come in, will be grilled to a crisp golden hue. The young apprentice tells me that he wants to run his own yakitoriya. He has a few rungs on the ladder to go.

At the other table a thin man with glasses is preparing *gombo*, the fatty, pyramid-shaped chicken tail, or what my grandmother used to call the "Parson's Nose." These too must be trimmed and cut to fit. The thin man is sitting on a cushion made from a phone book held together with packaging tape.

Behind the counter, Watanabe continues with his eels. It is about 10:30 a.m. "They'll bite you," he says, as he reaches behind him to haul another of the two-foot-long, cylindrical fish from its tub, which is filled with ice water to numb them. He lays out the eel on a cutting board that has a small hole drilled into one corner, and with the flat of his knife taps a heavy steel pin through the eel's head into the hole, to hold it steady, and then rapidly runs his knife the length of it, lifting a clean fillet from the tapered tail.

Now he works the knife in the same direction under the backbone, pulling it away before scraping out the remarkably miniature intestines, piling them at the top of the board. The liver, or *kimo*, is prized. It is skewered along with some white meat and sold at ¥300; the fillet meat—one skewer of which represents half an eel—sells for ¥1300. Morimoto serves about twelve eels a day. One of the other biggest sellers is chicken *sashimi*—eaten like raw fish, with *wasabi*, soy sauce and sometimes ginger and other condiments. It is creamy, rich and other-worldly. The chef in charge of it will arrive before noon.

An old, gray plastic radio, perched high on a shelf, burbles news and traffic reports as Watanabe, finished with his eels, cleans and stores the wooden cutting board and begins slicing onions for one of his most requested dishes, *tsukune*, or minced, skewered chicken. In minutes he has reduced a box of large white onions to a small mountain of translucent mince. He scoops the onions into a mesh cloth and squeezes out the moisture under running water. Then he takes a dozen or so quarters of frozen yellow *yuzu* citrus peel and trims off the remaining flesh before julienning and mincing them to the same dimensions as the onions. He tells me that he freezes the peel since the fruit is out of season. "But you can't freeze it in a domestic fridge," he says. "It will go black."

He then takes a heavy bag of chicken mince, empties it into a huge steel mixing bowl, adds the yuzu, onions, salt, and seasoning and begins the impressively physical work of kneading the mixture together. This takes around five minutes of powerful punching of his closed fist into the mush, and turning it. He speaks while he punches, explaining that he has been wary of being interviewed since a magazine accused Morimoto of using powdered, processed wasabi (the pub only serves the fresh-grated kind). But it's not as if Morimoto needs to care about what the media writes, since it turns away customers almost every night. In this age of celebrity chefdom, this lack of concern about promotion—a product of Watanabe's serious, artisan-like attitude to his work—is refreshing.

Watanabe is known to the staff as "shacho," the usual term for a company president, but his master, for whom the pub is named, is Teruyoshi Morimoto. Mr. Morimoto was born in 1928 and at the age of twenty began work at a small yakitori pub on the other side of Shibuya, before striking out on his own with this establishment in 1972.

Mr. Morimoto remains a strong presence, overseeing proceedings almost every night, dressed in his crisp white apron, wooden clogs, and twisted *hachimaki* cloth headband. The staff show him every deference you would expect for his age, and you sense a continuum from what the master learned so long ago through his apprenticeship. There is the old-style efficiency: no less than seven staff are on deck each night, and this for a pub that seats only two dozen. Service is extremely fast and customer turnover is high. No one who is not eating or drinking lingers; should you announce over your empty plates and glasses that you have had enough, you will promptly be presented with your check. This is a hold-

over from the old store, which seated only twelve or thirteen, and instituted a policy of moving customers on to deal with the nightly queues. "We opened in the late afternoon, which was when the local artisans and tradespeople would turn up. About 5 p.m. we would start to get the office crowd," says Morimoto, "so we had to make room for them all."

A *HAIKU* POEM discouraging lingerers has also been brought over from the old store, and two copies are pasted to the walls. It translates roughly as: *Let me share your branch to sit on/Sparrow in the night*. Along with another notice explaining more explicitly that it is bad form to hang around, customers cannot fail to get the message. But few are put off. Mr. Morimoto has a non-discrimination policy. In the old days the pub, which counts film industry and literary types among its regulars, displayed on its walls the signed missives of these celebrities, but Mr. Morimoto has done away with them. "I believe that every human being has the right to be treated equally, from the emperor to foreigners," he says. "I grew up playing with kids from Korea, so that's why I think this way."

Seasons affect the yakitori trade, with more customers flocking here during winter, perhaps to share proximity with the hot grill, fired with best quality, virtually smokeless *binchotan* oak charcoal, which Watanabe keeps glowing with a steady batting movement of the large, square paper fan in his left hand. Winter is also when wild birds come into season, since this is when they put on tasty fat, and between mid-November and February Morimoto serves pheasant, sparrow, little duck and male mallard duck.

But the steady favorite is the chicken

sashimi, and on the morning I spend in the shop, Mr. Morimoto's wife arrives to prepare it. She is also in charge of the *shiso-maki*, or rolled perilla leaf chicken, a yakitori standard that is rendered here to near perfection. From large hunks of fresh chicken breast she slices almost paper-thin sheets of meat that remind me of thick spring roll wrappers. She layers green shiso leaves on top of each sheet, then rolls it and slices it into three-quarter-inch-thick disks. These are skewered and, after grilling, smeared with crushed *umeboshi* pickled plums. As for the sashimi, she blanches the ingredients: chicken breast, liver, gizzards and so on, to kill any surface bacteria, then stores them in airtight containers to be sliced before serving.

To put it mildly, raw chicken is only for certain tastes, though on the many nights I have visited here, almost every diner seems to be ordering it. Despite the obvious risks—not least of them the advent of bird flu—it is hugely popular, and even breast meat that is grilled is usually served extremely rare, with wasabi. Since coming to Japan in 1988, I have never heard of anyone falling ill from chicken sashimi. But the specialist suppliers of this grade of meat have big reputations staked upon the safety of their product. The message is simple: *don't try it at home.*

As Mrs. Morimoto continues with her prepping, the other crew are busy with the rest of the skewering: heart, liver, gizzards, breast, wings, other cuts of meat and vegetables, all requiring meticulous trimming and preparation. Watanabe leans over the huge steel bowl and makes the tsukune mince into meatballs, with a deft and risky-looking scooping action utilizing a small triangular knife and a squeezing motion with his other hand. The meatballs

will then be flattened and pierced with two skewers. Most of the chicken here is generic, but Morimoto also specializes in two breeds—*Tokyo Shamo*, a fighting cock breed, and Akita *Hinadori*, both firm-fleshed and juicy.

At around 1 p.m. I leave the staff to it, because I have heard about their busy schedule from Mr. Morimoto: they will prep until 2 p.m., when they will have their staff meal—

probably based around off-cuts of chicken and vegetables in a miso soup—then from 3 p.m. to 4 p.m. they will take their "nap," during which time they may leave the pub to shop, or to smoke, or stay and sleep on one of the benches. I pledge to return in the evening, and I know the food will taste even more extraordinary now that I know how much care has gone into it.

PREVIOUS PAGE: a lineup of skewers, FROM TOP: *unagi*; chicken skin; duck and vegetables; liver; *tsukune*; hearts.

THIS PAGE: Producing quality yakitori is time- and labor-intensive. Master Watanabe works in perpetual motion throughout the evening, rhythmically fanning the coals and constantly rotating the skewers. He uses *binchotan* oak charcoal, which is extremely dense and makes a metallic ring when sticks are knocked together. Almost pure carbon, binchotan gives off virtually no smoke or odor and retains temperatures of up to 1000 degrees Celsius. It burns without flame, so that the yakitori is not scorched but gently cooked via infrared heat.

Once its head is secured to the cutting board by means of the steel pin, the eel is filleted and its backbone and innards removed. The unagi knife has a specialized chisel-like blade to get in behind the eel's triangular spine.

Preparation is in full swing from the morning. The white posters on the wall admonish customers not to linger, and to make room for others.

Minced Chicken Patties

つくね
Tsukune

I doubt there is a single secret to the deliciousness of Morimoto's *tsukune* patties, but one key may be the force with which Watanabe kneads his mixture, making binding agents unnecessary. Then again, it may be that these patties use meat from the whole bird, including ground cartilage. And the addition of *yuzu* peel is a masterstroke.

1 lb. (450g) ground chicken
  * A minced combination of chicken parts such as thigh, breast, neck, and gizzards will produce richer flavor.
½ small onion, finely chopped
1 tbsp. minced *yuzu* citrus peel or lemon peel
1 tsp. or more salt

Combine all ingredients in a bowl and knead thoroughly for several minutes. If the mixture is too sticky and soft, put in refrigerator to let firm. Shape into 8 balls. Using 2 bamboo skewers, with ⅛ in. (3mm) space between them, spread the mixture lengthwise along the skewers. Sprinkle with salt. Grill, flipping once, until the surface is lightly golden and the chicken is cooked through, for 15 minutes. Alternatively, cook in a toaster oven without skewers: flatten the ground chicken balls into ovals, lay on a foil-lined baking sheet and bake until the chicken is cooked through.

Ume-shiso Rolled Chicken

梅しそ巻き
Ume-shiso Maki

Another classic pairing of *umeboshi* sour plums, chicken and *shiso*, these use only lean breast meat. Take care to cook not too fast or slow, to prevent from drying out.

1 boneless chicken breast or 4 tenderloins, skinless
8 *shiso* leaves
Umeboshi plum paste (*bainiku*)

Butterfly the chicken breast or tenderloins lengthwise to make a large sheet of the chicken meat. Resting one hand lightly on the chicken, carefully cut horizontally into thin slices, about ⅛ in. (3mm) thick. With each slice on a cutting board, lay shiso leaves to cover and roll the slices into a spring roll-like form. Slice into about ¼ in. (6mm) thick rounds. Skewer the rounds crosswise onto bamboo skewers and grill until cooked through. Smear the ume plum paste on the grilled rounds and serve.

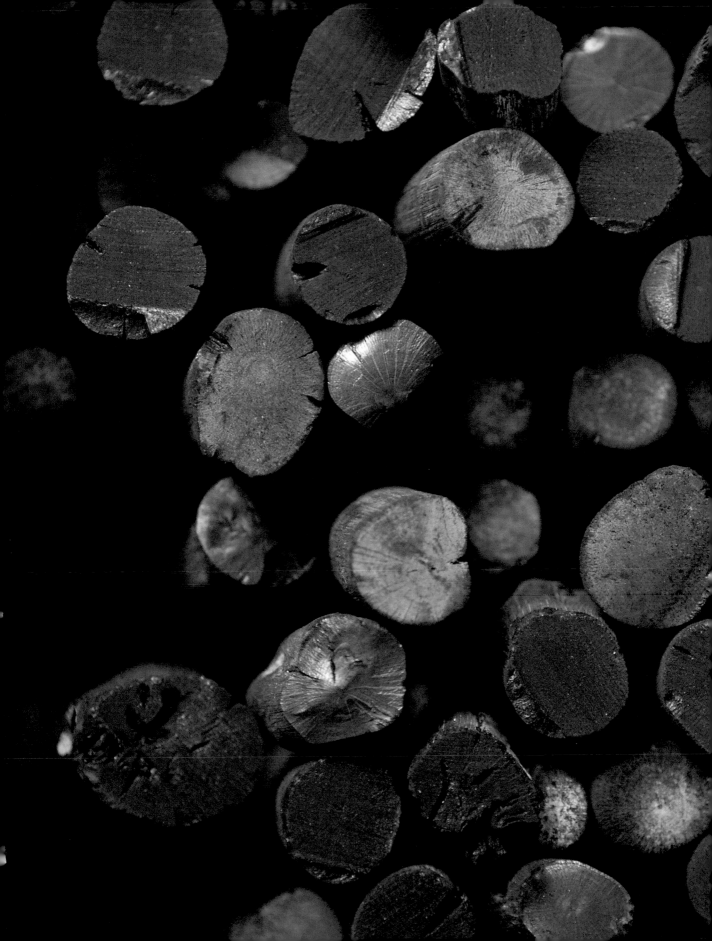

FUTURE
PERFECT

buchi

buchi Buchi

The traditional *tachinomiya*, or standing-bar, may not be everyone's idea of a good night out, but it has been an enduring cultural form. Packed with drink-flushed, upper middle-aged men, this relative of the modern izakaya is thick with smoke, starkly lit, and serves a limited, unremarkable menu. It is not made for comfort—as the name implies, there are few or no seats—and little care goes into the decor. Its defining aesthetic element is probably the upturned beer crate, stacked three- or four-high and topped with planks to make tables. I like this kind of "non-design design."

So I was skeptical when I heard about the emergence in Tokyo of a "new-style" standing-bar. Who would presume to repackage such a classic institution? No one could make the standing-bar grungier, so how sanitized would it be? Would it be like a chain izakaya—would it presage a new age of formulaic, franchise standing-bars?

The answer, so far, is no. The team behind Buchi—husband and wife Takashi and Hisae Higashii—took the original standing-bar concept and, as if it were a beer crate, stood it on its head to great practical and aesthetic effect. They made no attempt to copy the older standing-bar, though by employing a minimum of decoration, quick service, and low prices, and in a storefront barely ten-feet

135

wide (there is also a small downstairs seating area), they have captured the tachinomiya spirit. They have gone further, with a constantly changing menu of innovative European and Japanese small-dish cooking, and a wine list that would be impressive in a good restaurant. And if anything, by consciously making Buchi friendly to everyone, especially women (all the counter staff are female, and—more than just glowing with cheer—knowledgeable in everything they serve), they have simply updated the egalitarianism of the tachinomiya concept.

"The standing-bar used to be such an exclusively men's domain that women couldn't enter. We didn't think it should be like that," says Hisae. "Women should have places they can go to relax. If the place is full of men it becomes hard for women to enter, so we decided to make all the counter staff women. I think men are pleased with this too."

Hisae is a qualified sommelier and has the equivalent certification to judge *sake*. She is assertive and energetic, and shows an easy professionalism in overseeing her kitchen and hall staff, and it is clear that she communicates exactly what each member should be doing. She met and married Takashi when they worked together running an izakaya for another company. They were so successful they oversaw the opening of another seven branches, then quit when they realized that their jobs had become more about business than food. Buchi brought them back to hands-on food and drink service. "It's the sort of place we wanted for ourselves," says Hisae.

Buchi is certainly intimate—another word for it might be cramped—and though I am not generally a fan of standing for an hour or so as I eat, the layout and atmosphere make doing

so seem natural. The visual theme is simply corrugated sheet metal, glass, and honey-colored timber. There are no unnecessary flourishes, yet design touches such as hooks for customers to hang their bags under the counter top, and a well-placed foot rail, indicate consideration. Buchi's counter is a very comfortable place to be, and when I wonder if there is a particular reason for this, Hisae reveals the hidden thought that has gone into the establishment: "After researching other places we felt their counters were too low, so we raised ours four inches," she says.

BUCHI'S MENU draws on the Higashiis' passion for all kinds of food and drink. Takashi is Hiroshima-born (the name Buchi is Hiroshima slang for "very," he says, as in, "Very tasty"). It is not only their own interest that inspires a menu spanning sea urchin with scrambled eggs, *udon* noodles with sesame dipping sauce, porcini pizza, and char-grilled *jamon Iberico*. It is simply good hospitality, and therefore, smart business. "We can satisfy most demands, even for customers who come every day," says Hisae. "You could come here for a week and not get sick of it, it's non-genre. And when people come in groups, some might feel like Japanese food, others like French. We wanted to make it so that even if you're not sure what you want, you'll find something. And as much as we can provide is handmade."

The variety extends to the drinks, and Buchi has helped changed the face of casual Japanese bar culture by stocking *sake* in the famous "one-cup" format. In a 180ml (six ounce) glass with a ring-pull top, the one-cup sake, fortified with added alcohol, is the traditional cheap liquor for the working man. It is sold at stores and through vending machines, and has a downmarket reputation to match. But when Buchi started sourcing quality regional sake in the single-serve format, it attracted keen press and approaches from brewers across Japan. The standing-bar now stocks around thirty-five brews, with around twenty made exclusively for Buchi. Most of them, like the majority of the menu items, cost five hundred yen—Japan's largest coin denomination. This pricing policy has also influenced many emulators, so much so that the "one coin bar" has become a kind of byword.

The system also operates on a cash-on-delivery basis, and it's common to see customers settle themselves at the counter and put down two or three thousand yen, which will be their budget for the night. Change is provided in small steel bowls which act as paperweights on the bills. It is not so different from bar systems elsewhere, but was virtually unheard of when Buchi applied it in Tokyo. It is possible that the cash-on-delivery system may help mold Japanese social drinking into a more easygoing, individual form, as opposed to the often rigid, hierarchical rituals of traditional after-work drinking, in which everyone leaves together. "You don't have to wait for the check," says Hisae, "so customers come in when they feel like it and leave when they feel like it. At first some people didn't get it: some thought it was interesting, others that it was a nuisance. But now, even groups chip in to put their budget on the bar and go home when it's spent, or throw in a little extra if they want to drink a bit more."

Despite its now being a hugely popular Tokyo destination, Buchi did not take off immediately. It is a mark of the Higashiis' self-confidence that they chose a relatively incon-venient location, squeezed between an office block and a convenience store in the shadow of the Shuto expressway, then held out for ten months before customers began stopping by. Success put them on a roll, and in a few years they had opened four other izakaya, all variations on Buchi's efficient, friendly, and value-for-money philosophy. Each is notable for its clean, modern design and warm professional service, which suggests that the staff are well trained and looked after.

THIS FRIENDLINESS trickles down to customers, and spending an hour or two at Buchi can be a little like visiting a party. It is easy to exchange a few words with the stranger, or strangers, next to you. On one visit I find the counter is just crowded enough, and the glass front doors, the full breadth and height of the shopfront, are wide open onto the humid street. A couple of beer-crate tables have been set up outside on the edge of the intersection. I order a draft beer and a *goya* bitter melon and pickled cucumber salad. It is astringent, salty and refreshing. I scan the menu for something else, deciding tonight against the sashimi sardines and other Japanese influenced dishes, and opt instead for the very Western lamb chop, and a glass of New Zealand pinot noir.

The chop arrives off the char grill, plump and glistening, with three dabs of condiment on the side: a chili-citrus *yuzu-kosho*, a spicy miso paste, and a hot mustard. There is also a small mound of sea salt. The wine is deliciously chilled. Each item costs the standard five hundred yen. The chop gives off an irresistible aroma that turns the head of the young man in a printed T-shirt beside me, who has been locked in conversation with his workmate. He asks what I have ordered. We

Fried Whole Garlic with Miso

Here, spicy miso offsets sweet and creamy fried garlic. You can substitute scallions for *myoga*, and any variety of miso you like, though the Tokkara miso in this recipe is a mixture of miso, hot peppers, vegetables and bonito flakes. *Recipe p. 140*

Pu-erh Tea-glazed Walnuts

Famed for its supposed slimming benefits, pu-erh tea, from the south-western Chinese province of Yunnan, enjoys huge popularity among Japanese women. The tea is dark, comes in a hard cake, and has a distinct fermented aroma. You could also make these more-ish walnuts with Earl Grey, or a similarly distinctive tea. *Recipe p. 140*

fall into conversation and I learn that he is a computer programmer. He asks what I think of the different work cultures in Japan and the West, and I suggest the Western system may be better at rewarding initiative and individualism. He counters that the Japanese way is more weighted toward what's best for the company, and haggling over wages and stock options can seem vulgar. In a round-about way, I agree, as the thought brings me back to Buchi, where the staff do their abso-lute best with never a thought for a tip.

The Higashiis are successfully walking a fine line in taking the standing-bar in a new Western direction, and as much as they are food lovers, they are also entrepreneurs. I trust their intuition tells them that the way they run their stores and train their staff can only remain distinctly Japanese. I believe the tachinomiya is in good hands.

Fried Whole Garlic with Miso

揚げにんにく 自家製味噌添え
Age Ninniku, Jikasei Misozoe

P. 139

MAKES 1 head of garlic

1 head of garlic
⅛ tsp. sea salt
⅛ tsp. toasted sesame oil
Vegetable oil for deep frying
2 tsp. vegetable miso *see recipe below
2 tsp. *Tokkara* miso, store-bought, optional
1 *shiso* leaf, optional
1 *myoga* bud, thinly sliced, optional

1. Leaving the papery outer skin intact, slice off the top of the garlic head so that the cloves' insides are exposed. With a paring knife, pierce the cloves from the sides at their thickest part (so that they cook evenly). In a small pan, heat the vegetable oil to 340°F (170°C). Deep fry the garlic until the top is well browned and the cloves are cooked through, about 10 minutes. Drain excess oil on a paper-lined dish. While hot, sprinkle with salt and sesame oil.
2. Serve on the shiso leaf, topped with the myoga. Arrange dabs of vegetable miso and tokkara miso on the side.
3. To eat: Remove a clove of garlic from its skin, and dip in miso.

Notes: Tokkara miso is a fermented miso mixture with hot peppers, vegetables, and often with bonito flakes. It is a specialty product from the Shinshu area of Japan, which includes Nagano. Enjoy fried garlic with any local miso available to you.

Vegetable Miso

1 tsp. garlic, finely minced	**B** [*All ingredients finely minced:*
1 tsp. fresh ginger, finely grated	1 fresh *shiitake* mushroom, stemmed
1 tbsp. vegetable oil	⅛ small green bell pepper or ¼ Japanese *piman* pepper
	2 shiso leaves
	⅛ small onion
	⅛ medium carrot
A [½ lb. (230g) white miso	¼ tsp. minced *nira* garlic chives
2 tsp. Chinese chili bean paste	1 tsp. minced white part of a scallion or *Naganegi* white scallion
1 tsp. sesame seeds, toasted	
1½ tsp. sesame oil	
1½ tbsp. *sake*	
2 tsp. granulated sugar	

Heat the vegetable oil in a nonstick sauté pan and sauté ginger and garlic over medium heat until fragrant. Add **A** and stir well with a wooden spatula. Add **B** and lower the heat. Mix until vegetables are softened, remove from heat and let cool at room temperature. Store in a refrigerator in an air tight container.

Pu-erh Tea-glazed Walnuts

プーアル クルミ
Pu-a-ru Kurumi

P. 139

MAKES 2 cups

8 oz. (230g) walnut halves
5½ oz. (155g) granulated sugar
⅓ oz. (8g) *Pu-erh* tea
Vegetable oil for deep frying

1. In a sauté pan, lightly toast the tea over low heat until fragrant. Pulse to a powder in a food processor. Bring water to a boil in a medium saucepan. Blanch the walnuts for 1 minute and strain. Toss with sugar while hot.
2. In a large saucepan, heat the oil to 430°F (220°C). Have ready a baking sheet lined with a parchment paper. Deep fry the walnuts until the sugar caramelizes, for 4–5 minutes, then transfer to the baking sheet. While hot, sprinkle with the tea powder and toss well. Separate into pieces and let them cool completely. Store in an airtight container.

SAKE AKISHIKA

Buchi was one of Tokyo's first izakaya to promote premium *sake* served in the mass-market, "one cup" pull-top format. Akishika ("autumn deer") is an Osaka brewer specializing in *junmai* (no added alcohol) sake.

Whitebait *Nam Pla* Fritters with Garlic Chips

From the Mediterranean to the Americas, deep-fried white-bait is universal. Buchi gives it an Asian spin with the inclusion of Thai fish sauce. *Recipe p. 144*

Broccoli Rabe and Scallops Sashimi in Mustard Dressing

A quintessential, contemporary Japanese dish that should be assembled immediately before serving. Use the freshest scallops you can find. The bitterness of the broccoli rabe contrasts with the heat of the mustard. *Recipe p. 144*

Sliced Duck Breast with *Ponzu* Sauce

The ponzu sauce inflects this dish with a delicious citrus zing. The combination of hearty duck and astringent scallions are a perennial favorite in Japanese cooking.　*Recipe p. 145*

Whitebait *Nam Pla* Fritters with Garlic Chips

白魚ナンプラー揚げ

Shira-uo Nam-pla Age

SERVES 2–4

P. 142

2 large garlic cloves
4 oz. (110g) *shirauo* (salangidae) whitebait, or similar
Cake flour
Salt
Vegetable oil for deep frying

Nam Pla Marinade
½ cup (120ml) *nam pla* (Thai fish sauce)
2 tbsp. water
4 tbsp. granulated sugar
2 tbsp. Japanese pickled plum paste (*bainiku*)

A few *kinome* leaves, optional

1. For garlic chips: Thinly slice garlic cloves crosswise. In a medium heavy saucepan, heat 1 in. (2.5cm) of oil. On low heat, deep fry the garlic slices until lightly colored, about 10 minutes (the garlic will turn golden with carry-over heat). With a fine mesh sieve, transfer the garlic on a paper-lined plate. Sprinkle with salt while hot.
2. Soak the whitebait in the mixed marinade ingredients. In the same saucepan, add 2 in. (5cm) of oil and heat to 320°F (160°C). Remove the whitebait from marinade, dredge in flour, deep fry until golden and crisp. Drain excess oil on a paper-lined plate and sprinkle with salt while hot.
3. Arrange the whitebait with the garlic chips. Garnish with kinome leaves.

Broccoli Rabe and Scallop Sashimi in Mustard Dressing

菜の花と帆立の辛子和え

Na-no-Hana to Hotate no Karashi Ae

SERVES 2–4

P. 142

2 lbs. (900g) broccoli rabe *or* 1 lb. (450g) *nanohana* rabe
4 large sashimi grade sea scallops
½ tsp. Japanese hot mustard (*wagarashi*)
½ cup (120ml) *warishita* stock concentrate *see recipe below
Salt
A large pinch bonito flakes (*katsuo kezuri-bushi*), optional

1. Trim the rabe, reserving tender stalks, leaves and flower buds. Cut into 1½ in. (3.75cm) pieces. Have ice water ready in a bowl. Bring a large pot of salted water to a boil and cook the rabe until just tender but still crisp, about 3–4 minutes (nanohana will take 1–2 minutes.) Transfer to the ice water, drain, and lightly squeeze off excess water.
2. Horizontally slice each scallop into 2–3 rounds of equal thickness.
3. Dissolve the mustard into the warishita concentrate. Dress the rabe with ¼ cup (60ml) of the concentrate and the scallop, with another ¼ cup (60ml).
4. Arrange in a small serving bowl, and sprinkle with bonito flakes.

Warishita Stock Concentrate

MAKES about 1 quart

A ┌ 1 cup (240ml) soy sauce
│ 3 tbsp. tamari soy sauce
└ 1¾ oz. (50g) crystal sugar

B ┌ 1¾ qt. (1750ml) dashi stock
│ 1 dried *shiitake* mushrooms
│ 1 piece dried *kombu* kelp, 2 in. (5cm) square
└ ½ oz. (14g) bonito flakes (*katsuo kezuri-bushi*)

Combine **A** in a jar or bowl, seal and refrigerate for 10 days. After 10 days, mix with **B** in a pot and simmer over low heat until the liquid is reduced by half, about 1 hour. Strain through cheesecloth and let cool.

Sliced Duck Breast with *Ponzu* Sauce

鴨とネギのおろしポン酢

Kamo to Negi no Oroshi Ponzu

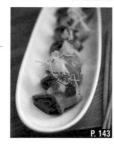

P. 143

SERVES 2–4

1 duck breast half, boneless, skin-on (about 12 oz./340g)
1 soft part of small leek or *shimonita* negi, with outer layer intact
1 tsp. olive oil
Ponzu sauce for marinade and sprinkling *recipe below
Salt and pepper

Garnish options

Grated *daikon* radish
White part of *naganegi* white scallions, sliced paper-thin
Chervil
Kinome
Sudachi or lime citrus
Yuzu-kosho pepper paste (*recipe below)

1. Preheat the oven to 400°F (200°C.) Trim any silver skin from the flesh side of the duck breast, and pierce the skin in several places. Rub the entire breast with salt and pepper. In a medium size oven-proof sauté pan, heat the olive oil until hot over medium heat. Add the duck, skin-side-down, and sear until the fat is rendered and the skin is golden crispy. You may want to soak up the rendered fat with paper towels or pour off the fat into a bowl for another use. Flip the duck breast over, transfer the pan to the oven, and roast the duck for 4–6 minutes, until medium rare. While hot, marinate in ponzu sauce for 3 hours.
2. Grill the leek with medium flame until the outside is a little charred and inside is soft. When cooled enough to handle, discard the outer layer and cut the leek into bite-size pieces.
3. Cut the duck breast diagonally into ¼ in. (6mm) slices and fold over the leek. Garnish with some grated daikon, scallions, sudachi citrus or other options.

Ponzu Sauce

½ cup (120ml) citrus juice, such as *daidai, yuzu, sudachi,* lime or lemon
½ cup (120ml) soy sauce
2⅔ tbsp. *mirin*
1 tbsp. *sake*
1 piece dried *kombu kelp*, 1½ in. (3cm) square
2 tbsp. bonito flakes (*katsuo kezuri-bushi*)
1 small dried *shiitake* mushroom

Mix all ingredients in a container and refrigerate for 3 days. Strain with a very fine mesh sieve.

Yuzu-kosho Pepper Paste

1 oz. (30g) *yuzu* citrus skin, bitter pith removed
1 oz. (30g) fresh hot green pepper, such as Serrano
1 tsp. salt
⅛ tsp. *shochu*, sake *or* fresh yuzu citrus juice

With a sharp knife, chop the yuzu skin and the green chili. Put in a food processor with salt and shochu, and pulse to a uniform but slightly coarse paste. Transfer to a small airtight container and let mellow in refrigerator for 10 days.

Scrambled Eggs with Sea Urchin and Lobster Sauce

This dish is triple rich, with the wholesomeness of eggs, the toasty, nutty fragrance of seared sea urchin, and the deep lobster sauce. Substitute ready-made homard sauce if preferred. Serve with toasted baguette. *Recipe p. 148*

Grilled Rice Balls with Vegetable Miso

Japan's *onigiri* rice balls are loved worldwide, but less well known is the grilled version. Crisp, light, and gently charred outside, they are fluffy inside and should be served piping hot. In this dish, the nutrient-laden miso-vegetable mixture is a popular "survival food" with mountaineers. *Recipe p. 148*

Goma-dare Udon

Chilled noodles, like hot *o-chazuke* rice broth, are a common finale to an izakaya meal. Here, the sesame dipping sauce is at the same time refreshing, cool, and rich. Thin *udon* noodles work best in this dish. *Recipe p. 149*

Scrambled Eggs with Sea Urchin and Lobster Sauce

雲丹のスクランブルエッグ
オーマール海老ソース

Uni no Sukuramburu Eggu
Omaru-ebi Sosu

SERVES 1

P. 146

1 large egg
3⅓ tbsp. heavy cream
2 tsp. butter
⅓ oz. (10g) sushi grade sea urchin
⅓ cup lobster sauce *see recipe below

⅓ anchovy fillet
Salt and black pepper
1 sprig of chervil, optional
Slices of baguette, toasted, optional

1. Mash the anchovy with the back of the knife. Season the lobster sauce with the anchovy, salt and pepper. Keep hot.

2. For the scrambled egg: Beat the egg in a small bowl, add cream, salt and pepper. Heat a 6 in. (15cm) nonstick frying pan over very low heat. Add the butter, and when it foams, pour in the egg mixture. Mix vigorously with a rubber spatula until the mixture is creamy. As the egg starts to set, stop mixing and distribute evenly on the bottom of the pan, and cook to your preferable consistency. Quickly slide onto a serving plate.

3. Brown the surface of sea urchin with a kitchen torch and arrange on top of the eggs. Spoon the hot lobster sauce around the edge of the eggs, and garnish with sprigs of chervil. Serve with the toasted baguette.

Lobster Sauce

MAKES about 1 cup

1 lb.(450g) lobster head
28 oz. (800ml) canned whole tomatoes
5½ cups (1350ml) water
3 tbsp. brandy
1 tbsp. olive oil
Salt

Heat the olive oil in a medium rondeau over high heat and sauté the lobster heads until well colored and just about brown. Remove the lobster heads from the rondeau and reserve. Add brandy to the pan and deglaze the bottom of the rondeau with a wooden spoon. Add the reserved lobster, tomatoes, water and salt. Simmer, stirring and skimming time to time, until the liquid is reduced to ¹⁄₁₀ of its original volume (about 1½ hours.) Strain through a chinois (cone-shaped strainer.)

Grilled Rice Balls with Vegetable Miso

野菜味噌の焼きおにぎり

Yasai-miso no Yaki-onigiri

MAKES 2 balls

P. 146

2 cups cooked short-grain rice *recipe p. 17
2 tsp. *warishita* stock concentrate *recipe p. 144
¾ oz. (20g) vegetable miso *recipe p. 140
Japanese pickles (*tsukemono*), optional

If the rice is cold, steam or microwave until hot. Mix with the warishita concentrate and cool enough to handle. Make sure your hands are washed clean and damp so the rice will not stick. Put ½ of the rice on one palm. With both hands, make a triangle-shaped rice ball about 1½ in. (3.5cm) thick. Repeat to make a second rice ball. Grill the rice balls over a medium flame until golden brown, then turn over. Spread the vegetable miso on the browned surface. When the other side is well grilled, remove from the flame and lightly scorch the miso with a kitchen torch. If using broiler, you can brown the surface of miso without a torch, but be careful not to let it burn. Serve with Japanese pickles, if desired.

Goma-dare Udon

胡麻だれうどん
Goma-dare Udon

P. 147

SERVES 4

10½ oz. (300g) *udon* noodles
1⅔ cups (400ml) goma-dare sauce *recipe below
2 *shiso* leaves, finely julienned
White sesame seeds, toasted
Kinome leaves, optional

1. In a large stockpot, bring 2 quarts (2L) water to a boil and cook the udon noodles until *al dente*, according to package directions. Drain noodles in a strainer and rinse well under running cold water to stop cooking and wash off excess starch.
2. Put the udon in a serving bowl and top with the shiso leaves and sesame seeds.
3. Pour the goma-dare into each serving bowl and garnish with the kinome leaves. To eat, dip udon in the goma-dare.

Goma-dare Sauce

MAKES 2⅓ cups

2⅓ oz. (65g) almond powder
4¾ oz. (125g) sesame seeds

A ⌈ 2⅓ oz. (65g) tahini paste ⅓ cup (80ml) *ponzu*
      2⅓ oz. (65g) white miso   * recipe p. 145
      ⅔ oz. (16g) Chinese chili   3 tbsp. soy sauce
      bean paste (*tobanjan*)   6 tbsp. *mirin*
    ⌊ 1 tbsp. grated garlic   6 tbsp. brandy

2¾ cups (650ml) *dashi* stock *recipe p. 101

1. In a small saucepan, bring mirin and brandy to a simmer to evaporate alcohol. Turn off heat and set aside.
2. Pulse the sesame seeds to paste in a food processor. In a heavy large sauté pan, lightly toast the ground sesame seeds and the almond powder. Transfer into a large bowl, add mirin and brandy and the rest of **A**. Pour in the dashi stock and mix well with a rubber spatula. The sauce should have a thick demi-glace-like consistency.

Hoppy, an old-time working class drink, has made a remarkable comeback among young Japanese drinkers. It is a low-alcohol (about one percent) beer-like beverage, made of malt and yeast, that is mixed with *shochu* distilled spirits. Depending on the establishment, the shochu may arrive as a sherbet-like, semi-frozen slurry. Simply mix the shochu (called *"naka,"* literally "inside") with the Hoppy, or *"soto"* (outside), to your preferred potency. Order more "naka," or "soto" as you wish. Hoppy is available in blond and dark styles.

The Way of Space

Japan's cramped conditions demand ingenious use of space, and few know this better than the chefs of small izakaya. From wardrobe-sized "cockpits," they turn out a cornucopia of dishes with stunning time-efficiency.

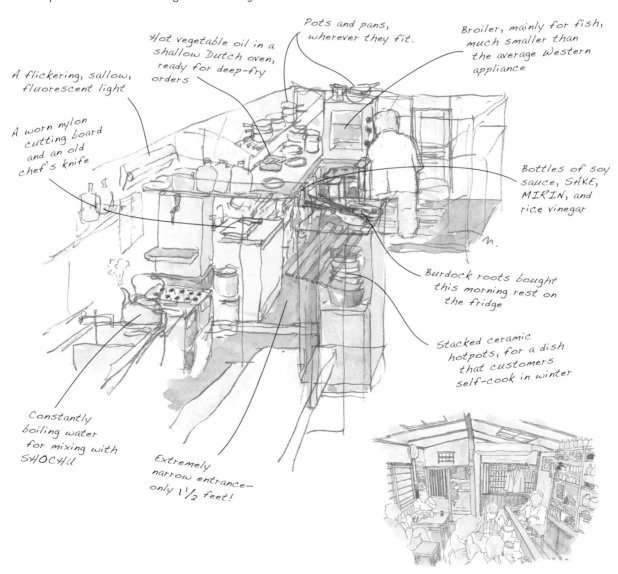

Hot vegetable oil in a shallow Dutch oven, ready for deep-fry orders

Pots and pans, wherever they fit.

Broiler, mainly for fish, much smaller than the average Western appliance

A flickering, sallow, fluorescent light

A worn nylon cutting board and an old chef's knife

Bottles of soy sauce, SAKE, MIRIN, and rice vinegar

Burdock roots bought this morning rest on the fridge

Stacked ceramic hotpots, for a dish that customers self-cook in winter

Constantly boiling water for mixing with SHOCHU

Extremely narrow entrance—only 1½ feet!

Talking Izakaya

The first thing that might happen when you visit an izakaya is that somebody will yell at you. This can be startling, as many establishments equate the force of a shouted greeting with the sincerity of emotion displayed. Thus you may encounter a heart-jolting "*Irasshaimase!*" (Welcome) to which a fair response is simply to bob your head and smile at your host, or say "*Konban wa*" (good evening). Once through the door, here are some words and expressions you will hear—in roughly chronological order, and by necessity oversimplified:

■ *Nanmei sama desu ka?* As you arrive, you are being asked how many in your party. Let your fingers do the talking.

■ *O-nomi-mono wa nani ni shimasu ka?* What would you like to drink? If one of you wants a draft beer, two want plum soda and one wants warm sake, order as follows: *Nama biiru wo hitotsu, ume shu soda wo futatsu, nuru kan wo hitotsu kudasai.* (NB: *kudasai* means "please.") Beer often comes in three sizes: small (*sho*), medium (*chu*) and large (*dai*).

■ To ask how much something costs say: "*O-ikura desu ka*?"

■ "Yes" is *Hai*; "No" is *Iie*. If you wish to catch a server's attention, call out, "*Sumimasen!*" This word is also used to mean sorry; i.e., when you've spilled your drink: "*Sumimasen deshita.*"

■ Many diners start with sashimi. If asking for a recommendation, say "*O-sashimi wa nani ga o-susume desu ka*?" But if the fish is on display, it may be easier to point. Alternatively, ask for a mixed platter, saying "*O-sashimi no moriawase wo kudasai.*" If you want to ask how much it will cost, say "*O-sashimi no moriawase wa o-ikura desu ka*?"

■ If the menu is all in Japanese, as is likely, you are best off either indicating what other patrons are enjoying, or asking for such items as those in this book (see glossary, p. 153). As each izakaya will have its own style, it is best to keep your requests fairly generic. You may also wish to leave your menu to the master. Saying "*O-makase shimasu,*" means "I leave it to you," though you may want to specify a price range, for example, "*Yosan wa, nomimono betsu de, yon-sen-en gurai de omakase dekimasu ka*?" (Can you make it within four thousand yen per head, excluding drinks?) Some inexpensive establishments offer "happy hours" that offer all-you-can-drink (*nomi-hodai*) or all-you-can-eat (*tabe-hodai*).

■ The word for "like," as in being partial to something, is *suki*. When asked if you like, say, pickled plums, you will hear "*Umeboshi wa o-suki desu ka*?" (The questioner shows politeness by adding "*o-*" to the word.) If you like something very much you will say of it, "*Dai-suki desu.*" ("Big like"). To hate something is to say of it *kirai desu*, though to say this of food could of course be insulting. Better to say, for example, "*Sumimasen. Umeboshi wa taberarenai desu*" (I'm sorry, I can't eat umeboshi).

■ To ask for the check, or bill, say either "*O-aiso,*" "*O-kanjo,*" or "*O-kaikei*" (they all mean the same thing) followed by *kudasai*. To get a receipt, say "*Ryoshusho kudasai.*"

Smile and give a bow as you leave, or even say "Thank you" in English, as this is of course understood. But everyone will appreciate hearing the correct phrase—"*Gochi-so-sama deshita*"—thank you for the meal. If all has gone well, as it most likely has, you will be accosted with a loud "*Arigato gozaimashita!*" (thank you very much), and depart, sated, with ringing ears.

GLOSSARY

For more on ingredients, see "Japanese Aromatics" pp.68–69

Abura-age Deep-fried tofu pouch.

Age-mono Common menu heading for deep-fried foods. Pronounced "ah-geh mono."

Akadashi miso A red miso soup mixed with dashi stock.

Bainiku *Umeboshi* plum paste.

Bakudaikai Scaphium. Seed of a plant found in Southeast Asia, used in traditional Chinese medicine, and in Japan as a *sashimi* garnish.

Beni-tade Tiny purple leaves with a peppery flavor. A common sashimi garnish.

Chayote A staple squash in Mexican cuisine and a viable substitute for *shirouri*. Known in Australia as choko.

Chazuke, or O-chazuke A hot and filling rice-*dashi*/green tea broth topped with various ingredients. [photo p. 27]

Daiginjo A type of sake, brewed with very highly polished rice. [p. 104]

Daikon East Asian giant white radish, a staple Japanese vegetable. See also **takuan** and **momiji oroshi**.

Dashi stock Essential cooking stock combining dried bonito or other dried fish, and *kombu* kelp. [recipe p. 101]

Deba knife Thick, heavy, knife for gutting and filleting fish. Like most Japanese knives, the blade is single edged.

Drop-lid *Otoshi-buta* in Japanese, it is typically a wooden lid smaller than the diameter of the pot and used to allow the ingredients in the pot to cook evenly without drying out or cooling. Can be substituted with aluminum foil, double-folded into a circle. [see recipe p. 20, 84]

Edamame Fresh green soy beans. [photo p. 23]

Edo Former name of Tokyo. The Edo period (1603–1867) is a divison of Japanese history marked by the rule of the Tokugawa shogunate.

Gobo Burdock root prized for its crunchy texture and earthy flavor. Rich in fiber.

Goma-dare Sauce made from sesame seeds. Similar to tahini.

Happo dashi All purpose dashi stock seasoned with soy sauce, and sometimes mirin. [recipe p. 36]

Hiraki Fish that is butterflied from belly or dorsal-fin side. Mostly used for *ichiyaboshi*, or overnight-dried fish.

Ippin ryori Literally "one dish cooking." A common menu heading under which you will find dishes that don't fit other categories, such as *age-mono* or *ni-mono*.

Jizake Regional *sake,* usually from small breweries.

Kaeshi A concentrate of soy sauce and mirin which has been mellowed over days or weeks. [recipe p. 117] It is commonly used in soba dipping sauce when mixed with *dashi* stock. See also **warishita**.

Kaiseki Japanese multi-course *haute cuisine*.

Kaiware Peppery sprouts of the *daikon* radish. Used as a garnish. [photo p. 66]

Kakiage A variation on tempura in which small-cut vegetables are combined with heavier batter and deep fried.

Kamo-nasu Round eggplant grown in Kamo, Kyoto region. [photo p. 47]

Katsuo, katsuo bushi, katsuo kezuri-bushi Also eaten fresh as sashimi, katsuo bonito is made into the rock-hard fillet *katsuo bushi* by boiling, dry-smoking and mold-curing. Dried bonito was once commonly shaved on a kind of plane called Katsu-bako [photo p. 101], but is usually bought today ready-flaked in plastic packs (*katsuo kezuri-bushi*)

Kinome The leaves of the *sansho*, the Japanese prickly ash tree, used as garnish. [see Shark Fin Aspic photo p. 98] See also **Sansho** pepper.

Kizami nori Slivers of *nori* seaweed, about 2 in. (5mm) long. Available at supermarkets. Substitute nori sheets crumbled by hand. [photo p. 119]

Komatsuna Mildly bitter, winter cooking greens with thick leaves.

Kombu kelp Dried *kombu* is essential in the making of *dashi* stock [recipe p. 28] and often used alone in simmered dishes to provide an *umami* flavor base.

Konnyaku A rubbery, gelatinous substance derived from the devil's tongue root. [photo p. 26]

Kudzu Known as "Japanese arrowroot." A climbing vine from whose root comes a starch used for thickening sauces or binding foods.

Kyuri Long, thin, tender Japanese cucumber. Pickling cucumber, English cucumber or Lebanese cucumber are substitutes. Eaten with skin on. [photo p. 66]

Maitake Wild Japanese mushroom. Grows at the foot of beech trees.

Matsutake Pungent mushrooms grown in red pine forests. They are notoriously expensive.

Mentaiko Spicy cod or pollock roe salted and seasoned with red chili pepper.

Mirin Sweet, aged rice wine used to season foods and give them a shine. Sherry is a reasonable substitute.

Miso A paste made from fermented soy beans, rice or barley, and a staple Japanese seasoning.

Mizuna Slim, crisp salad greens of the rabe family. Grown in the Kyoto region and often used in hot pot cooking.

Momiji oroshi Momiji are Japanese small maple leaves which turn bright red in autumn. The word is used figuratively to describe grated *daikon* radish (*daikon-oroshi*) when mixed with grated red chili. [recipe p. 20]

Nagaimo Mountain Yam A longer relative of the *yamaimo* mountain yam [photo p. 66], the *nagaimo* is less slimy and therefore not used as a binding agent.

Nanohana A leaf of the rabe family with edible tender stalks, buds and leaves. Its bitterness is prized in Japan as a spring green.

Natto Steamed and fermented soy beans. Very sticky, with a smell akin to aged cheese. Full of healthy enzymes.

Ni-komi A dish simmered/stewed longer than *ni-mono*. Usually utilizes the tough parts of meat.

Ni-mono Common menu heading for simmered/stewed foods.

Noren A fabric or woven rush curtain hung outside a store as an advertisement, to provide privacy, or protect from wind and sun.

Nori Dried sheets of laver, a marine algae, used widely in sushi and shredded as a garnish.

Nuta Green scallions together with shellfish or tuna, dressed with a sweet vinegared miso or mustard miso. One of the vast range of *ae-mono* dishes.

O-tsukuri A common alternative word for *sashimi*.

Panko Coarse breadcrumbs that when deep fried give food a lighter and crunchier texture than ordinary breadcrumbs.

Ponzu sauce A refreshing dipping/marinating sauce made with citrus juice, soy sauce and dashi stock. [recipe p. 145]

Potato starch Known as *katakuri-ko* after the katakuri plant of the lily family, whose root originally provided this pure starch for use as a thickening agent. Due to the increasing rarity of katakuri, the flour has been replaced with potato starch, though the name remains.

Pu-erh Tea Aged Chinese tea made by fermenting for years for a smoky, rich flavor. Believed to aid slimming.

Sakana The word for fish (魚), when written with a different character (肴), means "nibbles to go with drink," ie, izakaya food.

Saka-bayashi Green or brown globes made from cedar branches and hung outside sake-related establishments.

Sake Refers to alcoholic beverages in general, but also specifically to alcohol brewed from rice, fermenting agents and water: also called *nihon-shu*. [p. 102]

Sanbaizu "San" is three in Japanese: *sanbaizu* sauce consists literally of rice vinegar, soy sauce and mirin. Used like a dressing on shellfish or such dishes as Vinegared Wakame Salad. [recipe p. 16]

Sasagaki A shaving or whittling technique for tough root vegetables such as *gobo* burdock root. To shave burdock, take one end of the root in one hand, and rest the other end on a cutting board. With a sharp chef's or *usuba* knife shave the burdock away from you, as if sharpening a pencil. Plunge the shavings into vinegared water to prevent discoloring and to remove harshness. *Sasagaki* shavings have thinner ends than a julienne cut and become more tender when blanched. [recipe p. 44]

Sashimi Sliced fresh seafood or meat. Eaten with dipping sauce. [photo p. 43]

Shimeji Tasty, meaty mushrooms that come in a clump and are suitable for steaming or stir-frying. [p. 26]

Shiro Miso White miso. Fermented for a much shorter time than regular miso, has a mild and sweet flavor and retains the color of steamed soybeans. Used often in *kaiseki* cuisine.

Shirouri A summer squash suitable for making crunchy pickles. See **chayote**.

Shiso Perilla leaf. [photo p. 67]

Shochu Distilled white liquor, mainly from barley or sweet potato. Also the base ingredient in sweet *ume shu* plum liqueur [photo p. 10]. Shochu is made into cocktails by mixing with oolong tea, green tea, *ume* plum, grapefruit juice or anything you fancy. The name "chu-hai" comes from shochu and "highball" and generally refers to shochu mixed with lemon and soda, which is also known as a "Lemon Sour."

Soba Buckwheat, or buckwheat noodles. See **warishita**.

Soy sauce A staple seasoning or dipping sauce made by fermenting steamed soy beans, roasted wheat grains, water and salt.

Sudachi One of the Japanese lime-like citruses with a fragrant green peel. A speciality of Tokushima prefecture. [photo p. 66]

Sukiyaki A dish of thinly sliced beef and vegetables simmered in a mixture of soy sauce, sugar and mirin.

Suribachi Ceramic grooved mortar used with a wooden pestle for grinding foods. The pestling motion allows the easy extraction of oils from food, without cutting its fibrous cells and drying it, making a smooth paste. Suribachi range in size from only a few inches across to over one foot. [photo p. 34]

Takuan Yellowish *daikon* pickles named after a famous Zen priest. Often eaten with rice, or to accompany sake. [photo p. 39]

Tamamoto An emulsified mixture of egg and vegetable oil, used for making thick sauces in *kaiseki* cuisine. [recipe p. 44]

Tamari Wheat-free soy sauce.

Tare A rich, sweet sauce or dressing often used to flavor grilled meats such as yakitori. Variations on *tare* include sesame *goma*-dare, rice "wine" *saka*-dare, egg *tamago*-dare and so on.

Tsukemono, O-tsukemono, O-shinko Pickles. There are countless pickling techniques. Vegetables may be lightly pickled in salt (*asa-zuke*), more heavily in rice bran (*nuka-zuke*), in miso, soy sauce, sake, or mirin.

Tsukune Ground chicken, pork, or beef that is shaped into patties.

Udo Stem of Japanese spikenard. Similar to white asparagus in appearance and fennel in taste.

Udon Noodles made with wheat of a protein content between bread flour and cake flour. *Udon* also refers to the dish of udon noodles in soup stock.

Umami One of the five basic tastes, the word is most often used to describe a sensation of savoriness. Found in such diverse ingredients as dried kombu kelp, soy sauce, *shiitake* mushrooms, tomatoes, and Parmigiano-Reggiano cheese.

Ume Closely related to the apricot, the green *ume* is salted and dried with red *shiso* leaves to make the pickled *umeboshi* plum. [p. 57] Ume plum sake (*ume shu*), is often served with the green *ume* plum at the bottom of the glass, and is a popular izakaya drink. [p. 10]

Umeboshi Salt-cured plum. [photo p. 57] See also "*Ume*."

Unagi Freshwater eel. Served steamed or grilled with a thick, sweet *tare* soy-based sauce. [p. 129]

Usuba Very thin, single-edged knife for slicing or peeling vegetables. See **sasagaki**.

Wagarashi Japanese hot mustard. Substitute with hot English mustard.

Wagyu Literally, "Japanese cattle," *wagyu* is used to denote a breed of cattle whose meat is intensely marbled with saturated fat. The famed Kobe beef is one style of *wagyu*.

Wakame Fragrant seaweed most commonly available dried and salted.

Wakegi Wakegi green onions have a sweet flavor and a slightly slimy texture. They grow in bulbs like spring onions, while scallions, leeks and *naganegi* white scallions are grown from seeds.

Warishita Liquid made from soy sauce, mirin (or sugar) and dashi stock. For **sukiyaki**, it is used for simmering and seasoning. For *soba* noodles, it is used as a dipping sauce, after soy sauce and mirin only are mellowed over time (it is then called **kaeshi**) and then mixed with dashi stock. [recipe p. 144]

Yakitori Grilled skewered chicken.

Yanagiba Long, single-edged "willow leaf" knife for slicing sashimi. [photo p. 37]

Yuri-ne Edible lily bulb. Can be eaten raw, steamed or boiled Comes into season in winter. [photo p. 85]

INDEX

Bold type indicates an item that is contained in the glossary (pp. 68–69 or pp. 153–155)

A

abura-age, *see* deep-fried tofu pouch 153
aji horse mackerel
    Deep-fried Fish Cakes 44
    Overnight Dried Fish 60
akadashi miso 153
    Littleneck Clam Broth with Miso 101
all purpose dashi stock (happo dashi) 153
    recipe 36
    Deep-fried Fish Cakes 44
    Simmered Kamo-eggplant and Pork Loin 46
amanaga pepper 69
    Grilled Green Salad 100
Anaheim pepper
    as garnish 47, 56, 61, 64, 85, 120
    Grilled Green Salad 100
aonegi green scallion, *see* scallion 69
asari, *see* littleneck clam
asparagus
    Foil-baked Potatoes 44
    Asparagus and Pork Tempura Rolls 92
    Grilled Green Salad 100
atsu-age, *see* deep-fried tofu

B

bacon
    Japanese-style German Potatoes 24
bainiku, *see* ume plum paste 153
beef
    "Motsu" Beef Intestine Stew 95
bell pepper
    Deep-fried Stuffed Peppers 20
    Summer Scallop Salad with Spicy Tomato
      Sauce 93
    Grilled Green Salad 100
    Chicken and Vegetable "Nanban" Escabeche
      112
    Vegetable Miso 140
Black Sesame Sauce 76
bonito flakes (katsuo kezuri-bushi) 153
    Chilled Tofu 16
    Tempura Sauce (tentsuyu) 20
    Dashi stock 101
    Warishita Stock Concentrate 144
    Ponzu Sauce 145
broccoli rabe
    Nanohana Rabe and Wakame Seaweed Salad
      112
    Broccoli Rabe and Scallops Sashimi in
      Mustard Dressing 144
burdock root (gobo)
    Deep-fried Fish Cakes 44

butter
    Garlic Butter 64
    Garlic Herb Toast 95

C

calamari, *see* squid
carrot
    Pork and Vegetable Stew 28
    Mashed Potato Salad 81
    Chicken and Vegetable "Nanban" Escabeche
      112
    Vegetable Miso 140
celery
    Sautéed Small Squid and Celery 64
    Summer Scallop Salad with Spicy Tomato
      Sauce 93
    Chicken and Vegetable "Nanban" Escabeche
      112
chayote, *see* shirouri 153
chicken
    Deep-fried Stuffed Peppers 20
    Fried Chicken Gizzards 56
    Tatsuta Fried Chicken 84
    Chicken and Vegetable "Nanban" Escabeche
      112
    Grilled Chicken Breast with Ume Plum Paste
      120
    Minced Chicken Patties 130
    Ume-shiso Rolled Chicken 130
choko (chayote), *see* shirouri 153
cod
    Deep-fried Fish Cakes 44
    Fried Shrimp Quenelles 56
    Sweet Miso-marinated Fish 61
corn
    Fresh Corn Kakiage Tempura 47
crab
    Creamy Crab Croquettes 57
cucumber (kyuri Japanese cucumber) 69
    Vinegared Wakame Salad 16
    Ripe Tomato and Cucumber Salad 40
    Cucumber Pickles 81

D

daikon 153
    as garnish 37, 60, 120, 145
    Simmered Daikon Radish with Pork and Miso
      Sauce 20
    Daikon and Red Chili Relish (momiji oroshi)
      20
    Pork and Vegetable Stew 28
    Fried Chicken Gizzards 56

    Soy Marinated Daikon Peels 116
daikon radish sprouts (kaiware) 16, 20, 68
dashi stock 153
    recipe 101
    Sanbaizu Dressing 16
    Tempura Sauce (tentsuyu) 20
    Kombu Dashi Stock 28
    Horoyoi-style Rice in Dashi 29
    All purpose dashi stock 36
    Simmered Kamo-eggplant and Pork Loin 46
    Komatsuna Greens in Dashi and Soy Sauce
      64
    Black Sesame Sauce 76
    Chicken and Vegetable "Nanban" Escabeche
      112
    Mushroom Sauce 120
    Warishita Stock Concentrate 144
    Goma-dare Sauce 149
Deep-fried Eggplant in Dashi Marinade 64
Deep-fried Fish Cakes 44
Deep-fried Sardine Rocks 85
Deep-fried Stuffed Peppers 20
Deep-fried Tilefish 40
deep-fried tofu (atsu-age)
deep-fried tofu pouch (abura-age) 153
    Green Beans with Sesame Sauce 36
    Fried Tofu Stuffed with Raclette Cheese 80
dried kombu kelp 153
    Kombu Dashi Stock 28
    Cucumber Pickles 81
    Warishita Stock Concentrate 144
    Ponzu Sauce 145
duck
    Sliced Duck Breast with Ponzu Sauce 145

E

edamame 23, 69, 153
egg
    Deep-fried Fish Cakes 44
    Poached Eggs 92
    "Motsu" Beef Intestine Stew 95
    Omelet with Semi-dried Baby Sardines 116
    Scrambled Eggs with Sea Urchin and Lobster
      Sauce 148
eggplant
    Simmered Kamo-eggplant and Pork Loin 46
    Deep-fried Eggplant in Dashi Marinade 64

F

flounder 84
    Simmered Flounder, Edo Style 84
Foil-baked Mushrooms 28

Foil-baked Potatoes 44
Fried Chicken Gizzards 56
Fried Shrimp Quenelles 56
Fried Tofu Stuffed with Raclette Cheese 80
Fried Udon Noodles 117
Fried Whole Garlic with Miso 140

G
garlic
    Garlic Butter 64
    Garlic Herb Butter 95
    Garlic Herb Toast 95
    Fried Whole Garlic with Miso 140
    Whitebait Nam Pla Fritters with Garlic Chips
        144
ginger
    as garnish 16, 44, 85, 101, 117, 120
    Ginger Pickles 81
    Vegetable Miso 140
gobo, *see* burdock 153
goma-dare 153
    Goma-dare Udon 149
green beans
    Green Beans with Sesame Sauce 36
    Summer Scallop Salad with Spicy Tomato
        Sauce 93
    Grilled Green Salad 100
Grilled Chicken Breast with Ume Plum Paste
    120
Grilled Green Salad 100
Grilled nagaimo mountain yam 63
Grilled Rice Balls with Vegetable Miso 148
Grilled Whole Surume Squid 101

H
haddock
    Fried Shrimp Quenelles 56
happo dashi, *see* all purpose dashi stock 153
hoppy 149
horse mackerel, *see* aji horse mackerel

J
jako dried baby sardines
    Mizuna Salad with Jako Dried Baby Sardines
        85
Japanese cucumber, *see* cucumber
Japanese eggplant, *see* eggplant
Japanese hot mustard (**wagarashi**) 155

K
Kaeshi 153
kaiware, *see* daikon radish sprouts 68, 153
kakiage 153
    Fresh Corn Kakiage Tempra 47
Kamo-nasu 153
    Simmered Kamo-eggplant and Pork Loin 46
katsuo bonito flakes, *see* bonito flakes
katsuo kezuri-bushi, *see* bonito flakes
kikurage wood ear mushrooms 69

kinome 153
    as garnish 44, 84, 100, 144, 149
kizami-nori 153
    as garnish 21, 117, 121
komatsuna greens 153
    Komatsuna Greens in Dashi and Soy Sauce
        64
kombu kelp, *see* dried kombu kelp
konnyaku 153
    Pork and Vegetable Stew 28
kudzu starch 46, 154
kyuri japanese cucumber, *see* cucumber

L
littleneck clam (asari)
    Littleneck Clam Broth with Miso 101
    Spaghetti *con Vongole* in Japanese Style 121
lobster
    Lobster Sauce 148

M
mayonnaise
    recipe 81
    Fried Shrimp Quenelles 56
mentaiko, *see* spicy cod roe 154
miso 154
    Simmered Daikon Radish with Pork and Miso
        Sauce 20
    Pork and Vegetable Stew 28
    Sweet Miso-marinated Fish 61
    Miso celery 63
    Tuna with "Nuta" Miso-mustard Dressing 80
    "Motsu" Beef Intestine Stew 95
    Littleneck Clam Broth with Miso 101
    Miso-cured Tofu 117
    Vegetable Miso 140
    Grilled Rice Balls with Vegetable Miso 148
mitsuba leaves 69
    as garnish 29
mizuna
    Mizuna Salad with Jako Dried Baby Sardines
        85
    Grilled Green Salad 100
mushroom
    Foil-baked Mushrooms 28
    Deep-fried Tofu with Mushroom Sauce 120
    Spaghetti *con Vongole* in Japanese Style 121
myoga 69
    Fried Whole Garlic with Miso 140

N
nagaimo mountain yam 154
    Grille nagaimo mountain yam 63
naganegi white scallion, *see* scallion 68
nam pla (Thai fish sauce)
    Nanohana Rabe and Wakame Seaweed Salad
        112
    Whitebait Nam Pla Fritters with Garlic Chips
        144
nanohana rabe 154

    Nanohana Rabe and Wakame Seaweed Salad
        112
    Broccoli Rabe and Scallop Sashimi in Mustard
        Dressing 144
natto 57, 78, 154
nira garlic chives 68, 140
nori seaweed 154
    as garnish 21, 29, 117, 121, 153

O
Omelet with Semi-dried Baby Sardines 114
onion, red
    Ripe Tomato and Cucumber Salad 40
onion, yellow
    Japanese-style German Potatoes 24
    Skewered Pork Cutlets 60
    Onion slices 63
    Deep-fried Sardine Rocks 85
    Summer Scallop Salad with Spicy Tomato
        Sauce 93
    Chicken and Vegetable "Nanban" Escabeche
        112
    Minced Chicken Patties 130
    Vegetable Miso 140

P
panko 154
    Creamy Crab Croquettes 57
    Skewered Pork Cutlets 60
pickles
    as garnish 117, 148
    Asazuke pickles 63
    "Lightning Bolt" Shirouri Summer Squash
        Pickles 76
    Ginger Pickles 81
    Cucumber Pickles 81
    Chicken and Vegetable "Nanban" Escabeche
        112
    Soy Marinated Daikon Peels 116
piman pepper, *see* bell pepper
Poached Eggs 92
pollock, *see* cod
ponzu 56, 154
    Fried Chicken Gizzards 56
    Ponzu Sauce 145
pork
    Simmered Daikon Radish with Pork and Miso
        Sauce 20
    Pork and Vegetable Stew 28
    Steamed and Grilled Pork with Salt 37
    Simmered Kamo-eggplant and Pork Loin 46
    Skewered Pork Cutlets 60
    Asparagus and Pork Tempura Rolls 92
    Soy-flavored Spare Ribs 92
potato
    Julienned Potatoes with Spicy Cod Roe 24
    Japanese-style German Potatoes 24
    Foil-baked Potatoes 44
    Mashed Potato Salad with Mayonnaise 81

prune
   Spiced Prunes 80
Pu-erh tea 154
   Pu-erh Tea-glazed Walnuts 140

R

Raclette cheese
   Fried Tofu Stuffed with Raclette Cheese 80
renkon lotus root 68
   Ripe Tomato and Cucumber Salad 40
rice
   recipe for cooking rice 17
   Horoyoi-style Rice in Dashi 29
   Grilled Rice Balls with Vegetable Miso 148
rice vinegar
   Ginger Pickles 81
   Chicken and Vegetable "Nanban" Escabeche
   112

S

Sable fish (gindara) 61
sake 102–105, **154**
sanbaizu dressing 16, **154**
sardine
   Deep-fried Sardine Rocks 85
   Mizuna Salad with Jako Dried Baby Sardines
   85
   Omelet with Semi-Dried Baby Sardines 116
scallion
   Fried Chicken Gizzards 56
   Fried Tofu Stuffed with Raclette Cheese 80
   "Motsu" Beef Intestine Stew 95
   Omelet with Semi-Dried Baby Sardines 116
   Spaghetti *con Vongole* in Japanese style 121
   Vegetable Miso 140
scallop
   Summer Scallop Salad with Spicy Tomato
   Sauce 93
   Broccoli Rabe and Scallop Sashimi in Mustard
   Dressing 144
sea urchin
   Scrambled Eggs with Sea Urchin and Lobster
   Sauce 148
semi-dried baby sardines
   Omelet with Semi-Dried Baby Sardines 116
serrano pepper
   Yuzu-kosho pepper paste 145
sesame seeds
   Green Beans with Sesame Sauce 36
   Spinach with Black Sesame Sauce 76
   Goma-dare Udon 149
Shark Fin Aspic 98
shiitake mushroom, *see* mushroom
shimeji mushroom, *see* mushroom
Shirasuboshi, *see* semi-dried baby sardines
shirouri 154
   "Lightning Bolt" Shirouri Summer Squash
   Pickles 76
shishito pepper 68
   as garnish 56, 64, 85, 120

shiso perilla leaves 69, **154**
   Steamed and Grilled Pork with Salt 37
   Grilled Chicken Breast with Ume Plum Paste
   120
   Ume-shiso Rolled Chicken 130
   Fried Whole Garlic with Miso 138
   Goma-dare Udon 149
shochu 22, 25, 104, 105, **154**
short-grain rice, *see* rice
shrimp
   Fried Shrimp Quenelles 56
soy beans (edamame) 23
soy sauce 155
   all purpose dashi stock 36
   Soy-flavored Spare Ribs 92
   Soy Marinated Daikon Peels 116
   Warishita Stock Concentrate 144
Spaghetti con Vongole in Japanese Style 121
spanish mackerel 61
spicy cod roe (**mentaiko**) 154
   Julienned Potatoes with Spicy Cod Roe 24
spinach 34, 64, 92, 100
   Spinach with Black Sesame Sauce 76
   Grilled Green Salad 100
squid
   in sashimi 43
   Sautéed Small Squid and Celery 64
   Grilled Whole Surume Squid 101
surume, *see* squid
Szechuan pepper **68**

T

tahini paste 36, 76, 149
Tempura Sauce (tentsuyu)
   recipe 20
Thai fish sauce, *see* nam pla
tilefish 40
   Deep-fried Tilefish 40
tofu
   Chilled Tofu 16
   Deep-fried Tofu in Tempura Sauce 20
   Deep-fried Tofu with Mushroom Sauce 120
tomato 63
   Ripe Tomato and Cucumber Salad 40
   Summer Scallop Salad with Spicy Tomato
   Sauce 93
tomato, canned
   Lobster Sauce 148
tsukemono 155
   as garnish 57, 148
tsukune 130, **155**
tuna
   in sashimi 43
   Tuna with "Nuta" Miso-mustard Dressing 80

U

udo 155
   Tuna with "Nuta" Miso-mustard Dressing 80
udon 155
   Fried Udon Noodles 117

   Goma-dare Udon 149
umeboshi 57, **155**
   Grilled Chicken Breast with Ume Plum Paste
   120
   Ume-shiso Rolled Chicken 130

W

wagarashi Japanese hot mustard 69, **155**
   as garnish 60, 112
wakame seaweed 155
   Vinegared Wakame Salad 16
   Nanohana Rabe and Wakame Seaweed Salad
   112
wakegi green onion 80, **155**
walnuts 140
   Pu-erh Tea-glazed Walnuts 140
warishita
   Warishita Stock Concentrate 144
wasabi root 29, 43, 44, **69**, 112
whitebait
   Whitebait Nam Pla Fritters with Garlic Chips
   144

Y

yamaimo mountain yam 68
yuri-ne lily bulb 155
   Mizuna Salad with Jako Dried Baby Sardines
   85
yuzu 68
   Foil-baked Mushrooms 28
   Minced Chicken Patties 130
   Yuzu-kosho Pepper Paste 145

Z

zucchini
   Tatsuta Fried Chicken 84
   Grilled Green Salad 100

MAPS

HOROYOI

Yama Bldg. B1F, Ebisu-nishi 1-9-2, Shibuya-ku, Tokyo
Phone: (03) 3770-6405
Hours: Mon–Fri 5:30 pm–2 am (last order 1 am),
Sat and holidays 5:30 pm–12 am (last order 11:30 pm)
Closed Sunday
No English spoken, no English menu
Counter/table and floor cushion seating
Cards accepted
Appetizer charge: 400 yen

MARU

Aoyama KT Bldg. B1F, Jingumae 5-50-8,
Shibuya-ku, Tokyo
Phone: (03) 6418-5572
Hours: Mon–Sat 6 pm–2 am (last order 12:30 am),
Sun and holidays 6 pm–12 am (last order 11:30 pm)
English menu available, English spoken
Counter/table seating and private *tatami* rooms
Cards accepted
Service charge: 600 yen

SAIKI

Ebisu-nishi 1-7-12, Shibuya-ku, Tokyo
Phone: (03) 3461-3367
Hours: Mon–Fri 5 pm–12 am (last order 10:30 pm)
Closed Sat, Sun and holidays
No English spoken, no English menu
Table/counter seating. 2F *tatami* room can be
reserved for groups of more than five
No cards
Appetizer charge: 1,300 yen

SHINSUKE

Yushima 3-31-5, Bunkyo-ku, Tokyo
Phone: (03) 3832-0469
Hours: Mon–Fri 5 pm–10 pm (last order 9:30 pm),
Sat 5 pm–9:30 pm (last order 9 pm)
Closed Sun and holidays
Table/counter seating. 2F seats can be reserved
No cards
Some English spoken, no English menu
Appetizer & Service charge: 300 yen

YAMARIKI SHINKAN (Annex)

Morishita 1-14-6, Koto-ku, Tokyo
Phone: (03) 5625-6685
Hours: Mon–Sat 5 pm–11 pm (last order 10 pm)
Closed Sun and holidays
Counter/table seating (1F/2F);
Floor cushion seating (3F) can be reserved
No cards
Some English spoken, no English menu
Appetizer charge: 200 yen

HIRO

Tigris Naka-meguro II 3F, Kami-meguro
3-14-5, Meguro-ku, Tokyo
Phone: (03) 3714-8055
Hours: Mon–Sat 6 pm–2 am
Closed Sun
Table/counter seating
Cards accepted
No English spoken, no English menu
Appetizer charge: 400 yen

MORIMOTO

Hamanoue Bldg 1F, Dogenzaka 2-7-4, Shibuya-ku, Tokyo
Phone: (03) 3464-5233
Hours: Mon–Sat 4:30 pm–10 pm (last order 9:40 pm)
Closed Sun and holidays
Table/counter seating
English menu available
No reservations
No appetizer charge

BUCHI

9-7 Shinsen-cho, Shibuya-ku, Tokyo
Phone: (03) 5728-2085
Hours: Mon–Sun 5 pm–3 am
Standing bar
Cash on delivery
English menu available, some English spoken

Acknowledgments

Thanks to Greg Starr who injected vision and enthusiasm at the most crucial times; to Noriko Yokota for her belief, efficiency, and culinary wisdom; to everyone else who helped at Kodansha International and particularly the brilliant design team led by Kazuhiko Miki; and to photographer Masashi Kuma. To my family for their support: Mum, Hiroshi Shioi, my wife Luli, and my sister Gwen, who like the professional editor she is, anytime I asked provided penetrating insights. To Kun and Matto, who gave me somewhere to stay. And to the many others who shared with me their "special" places: Shigeru Yoshida of Cow Books, Kumiko "Soo" Suzuki, DJ Codomo, Toshihiro Sato, Kanmei Yano, Kentaro Moriya, Tetsuya Ozaki, Richard and Fiona, who first steered me to Maru, and the late Ed Seidensticker, an amazing family friend who introduced me to Shinsuke. For the positive energy, thanks to Kathy Bail, Simon Barney, Catherine Cheyne-Macpherson, and Jeanne Ryckmans. I also owe a debt of gratitude to izakaya writer and "guru" Kazuhiko Ohta, in whose footsteps no one in this field can avoid treading. Most of all I have to express my appreciation to the many izakaya staff and masters who gave their time and efforts, especially Keiji Mori of Maru, who provided the *dashi* and rice recipes, as well as preparing the *sashimi*, and to Kunihiko Saiki, who gave us the run of, and allowed our jacket shoot at, his historic establishment.

SOURCES

Gaunter, John. *Sake World*. 2004. John Gaunter.

Koizumi, Takeo. *Nihonshu Hyakumi Hyakudai* (Japanese Sake: 100 Tastes, 100 Facts) Tokyo: Shibata Shoten, 2000.

Kosuga, Keiko. *Kindai Nihon Shokubunka Nenpyo* (Food Culture Chronology of Modern Japanese Food). Tokyo: Yuzankaku Shuppan, 1997.

Morishita, Kenichi. *Izakaya Raisan* (The Cult for Izakaya). Tokyo: Mainichi Shinbun Sha, 1992.

Ohta, Kazuhiko. *Izakaya Douraku* (Izakaya Debauch). Tokyo: Shinchosha, 2006.

---. *Cho Izakaya Nyumon* (Super Izakaya Abecedary). Tokyo: Shinchosha, 2003.

---. *Seisen Tokyo no Izakaya* (Selections of Izakaya in Tokyo). Tokyo: Soshisha, 1993.

Ohta, Kazuhiko and Yasukuni Iida. *Tokyo Izakaya no Shiki* (The Four Seasons of Tokyo Izakaya). Tokyo: Shinchosha, 2005.

R. Froese and D. Pauly. Editors. *FishBase*. 2007. World Wide Web electronic publication. <http://www. fishbase.org/>

Yanagida, Kunio. *Japanese Manners and Customs in the Meiji Era*. Trans. Charles S. Terry. Tokyo: Obunsha, 1957.

（英文版）居酒屋料理帖　Izakaya

2008年1月　第1刷発行
2009年6月　第5刷発行

著　者　　マーク・ロビンソン
撮　影　　久間昌史
発行者　　富田　充
発行所　　講談社インターナショナル株式会社
　　　　　〒112-8652　東京都文京区音羽 1-17-14
　　　　　電話　03-3944-6493（編集部）
　　　　　　　　03-3944-6492（営業部・業務部）
　　　　　ホームページ　www.kodansha-intl.com
印刷・製本所　大日本印刷株式会社

落丁本・乱丁本は購入書店名を明記のうえ、講談社インターナショナル
業務部宛にお送りください。送料小社負担にてお取替えします。なお、
この本についてのお問い合わせは、編集部宛にお願いいたします。本書
の無断複写（コピー）、転載は著作権法の例外を除き、禁じられています。

定価はカバーに表示してあります。

© マーク・ロビンソン 2008
Printed in Japan
ISBN 978-4-7700-3065-8